the
Bean
Book

Rose Elliot is Britain's foremost vegetarian cookery writer and her books have won her popular acclaim in all parts of the English-speaking world.

Rose has been in the vanguard of the revolution in our eating habits in recent years, as more and more people consume less meat and take greater interest in healthy eating. She frequently contributes to magazines, gives cookery demonstrations and broadcasts on radio and television. Rose is also a professional astrologer and, with her husband, runs a computer-based astrological service which provides personality profiles, forecasts and compatibility charts. (For more details, please send SAE to Rose Elliot, PO Box 16, Eastleigh SO5 6BH, UK.)

Other Thorsons books by Rose Elliot

Vegetarian Christmas
Vegan Feasts
Cheap and Easy
Low Fat, Low Sugar

the
Bean
Book

ROSE ELLIOT

Thorsons

Thorsons
An Imprint of HarperCollins*Publishers*
77-85 Fulham Palace Road,
Hammersmith, London W6 8JB

First published by Fontana 1979
Published by Thorsons 1994
This edition published by Thorsons 2000

10 9 8 7

A catalogue record for this book
is available from the British Library

ISBN 0 7225 3947 9

Printed and bound in Great Britain by
Martins the Printers Limited,
Berwick upon Tweed

contents

Acknowledgements   vi

Preface   vi

Cheap Food, Good Food   vii

Nutritional Value   xi

A–Z of Beans   xiii

Buying and Using Beans   xix

Cooking Times   xxv

Soups   1

First Courses, Salads, Pâtés and Spreads   20

Bakes and Casseroles   50

Burgers, Rissoles and Savoury Loaves   64

Crêpes and Pasta   78

Pastry Dishes   91

With Rice and Cereals   101

Stuffed Vegetables   119

Top-of-the-stove Dishes   129

Vegetable Dishes   142

Basic Recipes   158

Index   163

acknowledgements

My grateful thanks to all the people who have helped, encouraged and advised me: to D. Driscoll of Stevens and Brotherton Ltd, for information on varieties and origins of beans; to Brian Wilmot, of the US Dry Pea and Lentil Council and to the American Embassy in London for helpful information; to J. M. Dent and Co. Ltd, for permission to quote from *The Englishman* by G.K. Chesterton; to Dr Alan Long of the Research Section of The Vegetarian Society (UK) Ltd; and especially to my family, for eating beans at practically every meal while I was writing this book.

preface

The Bean Book has made a lot of friends since it was first published in 1979, and I am delighted that Thorsons are republishing it in this new edition. Many people tell me that they discovered beans – and me – when they first left home and needed good food at rock-bottom prices. They could do no better than turn to beans, whose health-giving and nutritional properties are now much more widely known than they were when I wrote the book.

Beans and lentils are much easier to get now, too, and there is a range of canned beans as well as dried, to make life easier. You can substitute canned beans for dried in the recipes, allowing one 400g/14oz can for 100–125g/$3^1/_2$–4oz/$^1/_2$ cup of dried beans or lentils. It is also useful to know that if you cook 500g of beans or lentils then divide them into five equal portions, each will be the equivalent of one 400g/14oz can of beans. I put the cooked beans into small plastic bags and pop them in the freezer when I am organized, and use cans when I am not, but the dried ones work out cheaper. Anyway, whichever type you use, I do hope you will enjoy the recipes in this book.

cheap food, good food

According to archaeologists, dried peas, beans and lentils were among the first crops to be cultivated by man, and evidence of the remains of peas and lentils has been found in various excavations. Peas recently uncovered on the border between Thailand and Burma have been carbon-dated at around 9750 BC; others have been found in a Stone Age cave in Hungary and in the mud of the lake dwellings in Switzerland, dating back to the Bronze Age, about 3000 BC, while lentils have been discovered in Egyptian tombs dating from about 2000 BC.

Although our garden pea of today is unknown in the wild state, certain plants in Central Asia, the Middle East and North Africa are cross-fertile with modern cultivated ones and this leads to the belief that they originated in Central Asia, with secondary development in the other two places. It is thought that Aryans from the East later introduced dried peas to the pre-Christian Greeks and Romans and the latter brought them with them when they invaded Britain.

In the Middle East, lentils were certainly cultivated (probably from wild species that still grow in Turkey and other parts) by the ancient Egyptians, Hebrews, Greeks and Romans, and they are frequently mentioned in the Bible. According to Genesis 25:30–4 it was for a 'pottage of lentils' that Esau sold his birthright; in 2 Samuel 17:28 we read that David was brought 'beans, lentils and parched pulse'; and in 2 Samuel 23:11 a piece of land is described as 'full of lentils'.

The ancient Egyptians grew broad (fava) beans and they believed variously that the beans contained dead men's souls and were therefore unclean, and that they were the symbol of life and should thus be venerated and offered to the gods.

In Greece and Rome beans were used for casting votes when electing magistrates and other public officers. The beans were thrown into a helmet, white ones for 'pro' votes and coloured ones for 'con' votes. When Pythagoras forbade his disciples to have beans, he meant not that they should abstain from eating them, but that they should not take part in politics or 'love beans', that is, political office.

The term 'beans' also meant sexual indulgence – when Aristotle told his disciples to 'abstain from beans', he was not referring to their dietary habits.

These explanations perhaps enable us to read in a new light such statements as that of Robert Burton in his *Anatomy of Melancholy*:

That which Pythagoras said to his scholars of old,
may be forever applied to melancholy men,
'A fabis abstinete', eat no beans

and that of Donald Robert Perry Marquis in *The Almost Perfect State*: 'There will be no beans in the Almost Perfect State'.

During the feast of Saturnalia, Greek and Roman children would use beans for drawing lots to find out who would be 'king', and this association of beans with the feast of Christmas and the New Year can also be found in the old Western European custom of hiding a dried bean in a cake, the person getting this slice becoming 'king' of the revels. It is thought that originally the 'king' may have reigned for the whole of the twelve days of Christmas, his chief function being to perform the propitiatory rites to ensure good weather. In Italy lentils were traditionally eaten on New Year's Day to bring luck and good fortune during the coming year.

In the Middle Ages beans became associated with various spells and magic potions. For instance, it was believed that beans would cure baldness, and boiled beans mashed with garlic were taken for colds and coughs, a remedy not without virtue according to modern herbalists, but on account of the garlic rather than the beans. Nicholas Culpeper (1616–54) mentions beans in his *British Herbal*, published in 1653, advising that 'bean flour is used in poultices to assuage inflammations rising upon wounds'. He goes on to list various troubles: 'felons, biles, bruises or blue marks by blows, or the imposthumes in the kernels of ears', advising that beans 'helpeth them all'.

Before the end of the sixteenth century botanists in Belgium, Germany and England had written about and described many kinds of dry peas. But even a century later they were still a rare delicacy in France, fetching fantastic prices, though they later gained the reputation of being rather vulgar, as one seventeenth century writer remarked: 'It is a frightful thing to see persons so sensual as to purchase and eat green peas'.

Green peas also became associated with courting, and there was an old saying: 'Winter for shoeing, peascod for wooing'. This may allude to the custom whereby girls would place a peascod containing nine peas on the door lintel, in the belief that the first man who passed under it would be their future husband. William Browne of Tavistock (1591–1643) also connected peas with wooing in *Britannica's Pastorals*, II, 3, where he says:

The peascod greene oft with no little toyle
He'd seeke for in the fattest, fertil'st soile,
And rend it from the stalke and bring it to her
And in her bosome for acceptance woo her.

It's amusing in view of the traditional link between peas, wooing and fertility, to reflect that it was through his work on peas in the garden of his Augustinian monastery in Brünn in Austria, last century, that Gregor Johann Mendel laid the mathematical foundation for the modern science of genetics.

Many sayings involving beans and peas evolved over the years. From the late 1950s 'beans' has meant money (as in 'I haven't got a bean', etc.), but actually this meaning is derived from the French word *bien*, or 'something good'. The terms 'old bean', meaning 'good friend, good old thing', and 'to spill the beans' or 'to give away a secret', crept into the language later, the latter expression being American, but anglicized by 1928. As far as I can discover, the first time the expression 'full of beans' was used was in *Handley Cross* by Robert Smith Surtees, published in 1843, in which the description 'full o' beans and benevolence' occurs in Chapter 7. Then there is the old saying: 'He knows how many beans make five'. The right response to this apparently is: 'Yes, but how many blue beans make five white ones?' The correct answer is: 'Five, if peeled', to which one can only add a loud groan.

The word 'beans' is used in both French and English to mean punishment or retaliation, as in the old saying 'I'll give him beans', and the French proverb: '*S'il me donne des pois, je lui donnerai des fèves*' – 'If he gives me peas, I'll give him beans', or, in other words, 'tit for tat'. Kipling also used the expression 'give beans', meaning to defeat severely.

Then there is the saying 'as like as two peas in a pod', which was quoted by Lyly as long ago as 1597 in Euphues: 'as lyke as one pease is to another', and the old country belief that the perfume of bean flowers had an adverse effect on the brain:

Quand les fèves sont en fleur,
Les fous sont en vigeur.
(When beans are in flower, fools are in full strength.)

At least two words in modern use owe their origin directly to pulses (legumes). When the lens was discovered it was so-called because it resembled a lentil in shape; and the jewellers' carat was named after the carat bean. Because of its uniform size, this bean, which grows on the east coast of Africa, was used by the natives as their standard for weighing gold. This standard was later adopted by the Indians and applied to the grading of all precious stones.

Although pulses (legumes) have continued to play an important part in the diet of the poorer peoples of the world, in India, China and the Middle East, apart from wartime, when British housewives were urged to serve more 'body-building' beans, in the more affluent West they were neglected in favour of animal proteins, or simply grown as food for livestock. It's only in recent years, with worry about the increasing world population and food shortages, that these foods have received more serious attention.

nutritional value

But since he stood for England
And knew what England means,
Unless you give him bacon,
You must not give him beans.

So said G.K. Chesterton in *The Englishman* and, indeed, that's what many people used to think. But, as I've already explained, beans without bacon are perfectly acceptable, even to Englishmen, and can certainly stand on their own as the main dish of the meal. But all the pulses (legumes) are versatile, being equally at home in soups, first courses and salads, as well as substantial main dishes, as the recipes in this book demonstrate.

It's only in recent years that we've come to realize the full nutritional value of pulses (legumes). They used to be dismissed as 'second-class protein', and even in wartime advertisements, when the British government wanted to encourage their use, they were said to be 'body-builders, though not quite as good as fish', while fish was only described as being 'practically equal to meat', which put the beans quite a long way down the scale. However, since then, our understanding of protein has changed and we no longer think of protein as being 'first class' or 'second class'. We now know that there are different types of protein, and that if you put these different types together they complement each other to give full nutritional value. While pulse (legume) protein is valuable in its own right, it can be made all the more so by eating protein from another group on the same day. These other groups which complement pulse (legume) protein are grains, nuts, seeds, eggs and milk, including milk products such as cheese.

Mixing proteins often happens naturally in a meal. For instance, baked beans are usually served on toast, and it's very normal to serve lentil soup with bread, in both cases bringing together complementary proteins. I think it is interesting how many traditional peasant pulse (legume) dishes provide this complementary balance of protein. Indian dals, for instance, are made from pulses (legumes) and are nearly always served with rice or a chapati made from wheat. Even nature seems to encourage this, too, because, agriculturalists tell me, rice and legumes are excellent crops to follow each other in rotation. The mixture of cereal and pulse (legume) protein is found in a number of traditional Italian recipes, such as the popular *tuoni e lampo* or 'thunder and lightning', in which chick peas are served with vermicelli, and in the Middle Eastern felafel, or little chick pea rissoles, which are eaten with Arab bread. It's interesting, too, that in both the Middle East and India, where so many pulses (legumes) are eaten, yogurt, another food which complements pulse (legume) protein, is extremely popular. But I think perhaps the most fascinating example of the natural blending of the complementary proteins in a peasant dish is hummus, that creamy dip of puréed chick peas and tahini, or sesame cream, which is enjoyed throughout the Middle East. However, pulses (legumes) offer valuable and plentiful protein whether or not you mix them with foods from other food groups.

Some people I know avoid serving pulses (legumes) because they share the sentiment expressed in Edward Lear's limerick:

There was an old person of Dean,
Who dined on one pea and one bean;
For he said. 'More than that,
Would make me too fat,'
That cautious old person of Dean.

One Hundred Nonsense Pictures and Rhymes

This caution is somewhat misplaced, however, especially if pulses (legumes) are being served as a main course. According to *The Composition of Foods* by McCance and Widdowson, they contain only about 80 calories per 25g/1oz dry weight, and 100–125g/ 3½–4oz/½ cup provides an ample course for anyone, with only half or a third of that quantity needed if they're being served alongside other protein. And as well as containing protein, they're a good source of iron, phosphorus and B vitamins. In addition, they have the lowest fat content of any of the protein foods and their fibre content is extremely high, both important factors from the health point of view. The high-fibre, high-carbohydrate content means that we absorb their energy slowly and steadily over several hours.

a–z of beans

ADZUKI BEANS

These are small, reddish-brown beans, rounded in shape with a point at one end. They have a strong, nutty, sweet flavour, and are much used in the macrobiotic diet, because, as Eunice Farmilant says in *Macrobiotic Cooking*, they are 'the most yang beans'. They probably originate from China. In the Orient, adzuki beans are usually cooked to a rather soft consistency and served with such ingredients as coconut milk. They are also cooked with rice, their bright colour tinting the rice an attractive pink, as in the Japanese dish, Red-Cooked Festival Rice. In the East it's also common to find adzuki beans sweetened with sugar and made into cakes and sweetmeats.

BLACK BEANS

Members of the kidney bean family, black beans are large and shiny and much used in Caribbean cookery. One popular black bean dish from Cuba is called 'Moors and Christians', and consists of black beans cooked with rice and spices, black against white. Like all the kidney beans, they cook to a deliciously succulent texture and are particularly attractive when mixed with other beans to give colour contrast in casseroles and salads. You can substitute black beans for red kidney beans in any of the recipes in this book.

BLACK EYED BEANS

Also referred to as black eyed peas, or cow peas, black eyed beans are a variety of cow pea. They are smaller than black beans, creamy coloured and kidney shaped, with a distinctive black spot or 'eye' on them, hence their name. Black eyed beans are one of the quicker cooking pulses, and they have a pleasant, savoury flavour and succulent texture. They can be used as a substitute for haricot (navy), butter or lima beans.

BORLOTTI BEANS

These beans are variously known as borlotti, borletti, salugia, crab-eye and rose cocoa beans. They are kidney shaped and range in colour from a pale, creamy pink to a deep, brownish pink, and are attractively speckled. The best are the pale ones. When cooked, they have a tender, moist texture and a sweetish, very pleasant flavour. Borlotti beans belong to the kidney bean family and can be used in any recipe in place of kidney or haricot (navy) beans.

BROAD (FAVA) BEANS

Familiar to most gardeners, broad (fava) beans are flat and kidney shaped, with a hard, brownish skin. The skin is tough, and so needs to be removed before the beans are served, although sometimes these beans can be bought – more expensively – skinned. The broad (fava) bean grows in many countries all over the world, but they're not always easy to obtain – try Greek stores.

BUTTER BEANS

These are one of the largest beans, flattish, kidney shaped and creamy white in colour. I find them very useful: they can be served simply as a vegetable or part of a salad but are particularly good in curries, casseroles, pies and hotpots. They need careful cooking so that they are tender but not mushy. See also LIMA BEANS.

CANNELLINI BEANS

Sometimes called fazolia beans, cannellini beans look like small white kidney beans, and indeed are a member of that family. They can be used in any recipe calling for ordinary white haricot (navy) beans.

CHICK PEAS

Also called garbanzo beans and ceci, and native to Asia, chick peas are a great favourite in Middle Eastern and Mediterranean cookery, as well as in India, where they are known as *gram*. In appearance they look like rather small, dry hazelnuts and are light golden brown in colour. They retain their shape well when cooked and have a particularly appetizing aroma and taste. I think they are one of the most useful and delicious pulses (legumes).

FAVA BEANS, see BROAD BEANS

FLAGEOLET BEANS

Flageolet beans are pale green in colour and long and slim in shape. They are in fact haricot (navy) beans which have been removed from the pod while still young and tender, which accounts for their delicate green colour, tender texture – and high price. Although something of an extravagance, they make a very pretty salad for a special occasion and are also a particularly attractive addition to any bean mixture, because of their unusual colour. They are not as easy to find as some of the other beans: try health food stores.

The name flageolet, incidentally, relates to the fact that the French thought they looked like a flute, or *flageolet*.

FUL MEDAMES BEANS

These beans, which come from Egypt, are smallish, round in shape and brown in colour. They have rather a tough outer skin and so need careful cooking, but when they are soft they have a pleasant, earthy flavour. They are very popular in the Middle East, where, flavoured with garlic, olive oil and lemon juice, they can be served at any meal of the day, including breakfast. Look for them in specialist Middle Eastern stores.

GARBANZO BEANS, see CHICK PEAS

HARICOT (NAVY) BEANS

Small and oval in shape, creamy white in colour, haricot (navy) beans are a variety of kidney bean and are familiar to most people. They originate from Central and South America, being brought to Europe in the sixteenth century. They became known as haricot beans because the French included them in their stews or *haricots*. Their American name, navy beans, was apparently coined by Commodore Perry while he was eating them one day in Lake Erie during a British assault.

Although they're probably best known in the form of baked beans, haricot (navy) beans can be prepared in many delicious ways and are one of the most useful and easily obtainable of the pulses (legumes).

LENTILS, GREEN, BROWN AND PUY

Unlike split red lentils and split peas, these lentils retain their shape after cooking and are therefore useful when you want to give textural interest to a dish. They are interchangeable in recipes, but the French Puy lentils, which are a little smaller than the others, are the quickest cooking and tastiest.

LENTILS, SPLIT RED

Sometimes referred to as Egyptian lentils, split red lentils are the bright orange-red ones which can be obtained from most supermarkets. They cook quickly to a light golden-beige and they do not need to be soaked first, although this does speed up their cooking time even more. They have a particularly pleasant, bland flavour, but they do not hold their shape, cooking to a soft mass.

In Indian recipes, split red lentils can be used to replace masur dal, though botanists disagree as to whether or not these two are the same species.

LIMA BEANS

Native to tropical America, and called Lima because that is where the original seeds came from, these beans are sometimes called 'the aristocrat of the bean family'. They are rather like butter beans in appearance and are indeed referred to as butter beans in the southern USA. They have a lovely sweet flavour on account of their high sugar content. Unfortunately, they are not easy to obtain in the UK.

MUNG BEANS

Probably best known in their sprouted form as bean sprouts, mung beans are small, round and green and can be cooked like any other pulse (legume). In fact they are one of the quicker cooking pulses (legumes) and have a rather sweet flavour and soft texture. They can be cooked without soaking.

Native to India, mung beans are grown throughout Africa, China, the US and India itself, where they are known as *mung dal*.

NAVY BEANS, see HARICOT BEANS

PEAS

Looking like pale, wizened versions of fresh peas, dried peas (or soup peas as they are called in the US), cook to the familiar mushy peas of school days, but imaginatively cooked, they can be quite tasty, with their pleasant sweet flavour.

PINTO BEANS

Pinto beans are medium-sized and look rather like borlotti beans, with brown specks; in fact pinto means 'speckled'. They are yet another variety of the kidney bean and have a delicious savoury flavour and pink colour when they're cooked.

RED KIDNEY BEANS

Rich red in colour and with the characteristic kidney shape, red kidney beans are one of the most attractive of beans. They cook to a deliciously 'mealy' texture and are excellent both in salads and substantial dishes. They are much used in South America and the Caribbean, and also in India, where they are known as *rajma dal*.

SOYA BEANS

Originating in eastern Asia, and known and valued by the Chinese for thousands of years, soya beans (soybeans) have the highest protein content of any of the pulses (legumes) and are small, round and yellowish-brown in colour. They are the hardest beans and, in their natural state, they need a long soak followed by several hours' cooking and then careful seasoning to make them palatable. However, a partially cooked variety known as soya 'splits' is available, and this cooks in about 30 minutes without soaking.

Soya beans (soybeans) are also well known in their other form, as soya flour, which is soft, pale yellow and very rich in protein. The flour is useful for increasing the protein value of other foods, where this is a problem; it can also be used to make non-dairy milks and two types of 'cheese', which is useful for people who are allergic to these foods or who prefer not to eat dairy produce. One of the soya cheeses, bean curd or tofu, is widely used in Chinese cookery. Fresh tofu can be bought in stores specializing in Chinese foods or serving a large Chinese community. Packaged tofu can be bought in most supermarkets and health food stores.

SPLIT PEAS

These, as their name suggests, are peas which have been split in half, their outer skin having been removed. Both yellow and green varieties are available, although the latter are not so easy to find.

Split peas have a pleasant, slightly sweet flavour, but, like split red lentils, do not hold their shape, disintegrating as they soften.

buying and using beans

It's pleasant buying pulses (legumes) because they're so attractive, with their shiny appearance and bright colours. Lovely, too, to find an ever-increasing variety becoming available in supermarkets as well as health food stores.

Although dried beans, peas and lentils are easy-going in that they can be stored on the shelf and do not perish easily, it is a mistake to think that they can be left at the back of the storecupboard for months and months. Long storage can harden them to the extent that no amount of cooking will make them tender. For this reason, it is best to buy them in fairly small quantities from a store with a quick turnover, as you need them.

EQUIPMENT

The equipment needed for pulse (legume) cookery is really simple and straightforward, and you probably already have everything you need in your kitchen. You need a large sieve (strainer) in which to put the pulses (legumes) when washing and rinsing them; a large china or glass bowl in which to soak them; and a medium to large heavy-based saucepan for cooking them in. I think the heavy cast-iron casseroles, which can be used either on top of the stove or in the oven, are ideal for pulses (legumes). One or two of these in different sizes, plus a 900ml /1½ pint/3¾ cup and a 1.75 litre/3 pint /3¾ pint shallow oblong ovenproof dish should cater for most needs.

A pressure cooker is very useful because pulses (legumes) take a minimum of 20–30 minutes and usually nearer an hour or more to cook, and a pressure cooker can reduce this by about two-thirds. A little care and experimentation is necessary though, because it's quite easy to overcook some of the pulses (legumes), such as butter or lima beans and black eyed beans (peas), and reduce their lovely texture to a soft mush.

At the other end of the scale, one of those slow-cooking pots, which cooks food very gently for several hours on a small amount of electricity, is also excellent for cooking pulses (legumes).

I also use a food processor or blender a good deal in pulse (legume) cookery, particularly for soups.

Dishes made from pulses (legumes) have a homely quality about them, a comforting, rather earthy charm which can be enhanced by serving them simply, in chunky pottery. Presented attractively in this way and produced with a flourish – and certainly no apology – pulses (legumes) have a very basic appeal, perhaps in view of the generations they have sustained, evoking archetypal memories, but certainly physically and aesthetically satisfying.

PREPARATION

Nicholas Culpeper, writing in the seventeenth century, called beans 'extremely windy meat', an opinion which I know is widely held today, and certainly discourages some people from trying them. I have found, however, that the digestibility of pulses (legumes) depends to quite a large extent on how they are prepared and cooked. When Culpeper goes on to say, 'but if after the Dutch fashion, when they are half boiled you husk them and stew them (I cannot tell you how, for I never was a cook in all my life) they are wholesome food', I think he was on to something, because the secret seems to lie in rinsing – and sometimes parboiling and rinsing – the beans after they've been soaked.

I asked Dr Alan Long of the Research Section of The Vegetarian Society (UK) Ltd whether there was any scientific basis for the 'indigestibility' of pulses (legumes) and, if so, whether this could really be modified by the method of preparation. This was his reply:

Many cereals and pulses contain anti-nutritional factors which are removed in the processing, as in soaking, cooking, fermenting or sprouting. Some pulses contain as many as seven such factors. Some of these, such as cyanogenic substances (which decompose and liberate small amounts of hydrocyanic acid or prussic acid, which are boiled off) are of little concern in Western cuisines, but the enzyme inhibitors, notably of the digestive enzyme trypsin, are important. These are proteins, denatured, or otherwise inactivated, by soaking, sprouting, fermenting or cooking.

Such processes, which operate faster on thin-skinned beans and peas, also modify the starches, just as those in potatoes are made digestible. However, beans contain some unusual saccharides, notably raffinose, stachyose and verbascose, that may not be reduced in the fore-gut to metabolizable and absorbable sugars (as monosaccharides), so they enter the large intestine, where bacteria (which have prodigious powers of digestion) consume them, liberating carbon dioxide, hydrogen and methane (which are gases) and acetic and other acids. Evolution of these gases causes flatulence. It seems likely that we adapt in these ways to the pulse-saccharides:

1. We develop the required enzymic activity in the stomach and small intestine. This possibility seems remote, although we have adapted to life-long consumption of milk-sugar for which the 'natural' digestive system survives for only a few years after weaning;
2. The flora in the large intestine lacks bacteria capable of breaking down the stachyose, etc., so they pass out unchanged;
3. The large intestines of people who can digest pulses contain bacteria which convert the saccharides into mainly non-gaseous metabolites (e.g. generating propionic rather than acetic acid). There are certain genetic differences in people's reactions to the components of beans. The metabolism of ruminants can be altered in this way;
4. Social customs allow unexceptionable relief of wind, thus reducing pressure and discomfort in the sigmoid colon. The horse avails itself effectively of this ability.

The gastric motility induced by beans probably represents a beneficial effect, especially as so many people's diets lack in fibre. Anyway, you can be sure your culinary tricks with beans represent good nutritional sense.

In view of what Dr Long says, if you have trouble digesting pulses (legumes), I think it would certainly be worth taking extra care with the preparation, and possibly concentrating on the thinner-skinned varieties – you can tell which these are by looking at the table of cooking times on page xxv; the thinner the skin, the more quickly they cook.

Anyway, here's the method of preparation that I've found works. Basically it consists of four processes: washing, soaking, rinsing and cooking, with an optional extra parboiling-and-rinsing before the final cooking if you find it's necessary to make them digestible for you.

WASHING

Pulses (legumes) may be in greater or lesser need of washing depending on how and where they were bought, although I like to swish even the pre-packed ones from the supermarket in some cold water before using them. If the pulses (legumes) look very dusty, I think it's best to put them first into a bowl of cold water, swirl them round well and check for any foreign bodies such as the odd bit of stick or stone. Then put them into a large sieve (strainer) and run some cold water through them, moving them around with your fingers to make sure that the water gets to them all. Cleaner pulses (legumes) can just be rinsed in the sieve (strainer).

SOAKING

There's no doubt that most pulses (legumes) benefit from an initial soaking before cooking. This not only speeds up the subsequent cooking time but also helps to make them more digestible. There are two ways of soaking:

1. The long cold soak, which means covering the pulses (legumes) with twice their volume in cold water and leaving them to soak for 4–8 hours, or overnight.
2. The short hot soak, which is a boon if you've forgotten to get organized in advance. For this method, you simply put the washed pulses (legumes) into a saucepan, cover them with plenty of cold water and bring them to the boil. Let them boil vigorously for 2–3 minutes, then remove them from the heat, cover the saucepan and leave them to soak for 45–60 minutes.

RINSING

After they've soaked, it helps to make the pulses (legumes) more digestible if you then put them into a large sieve (strainer) and rinse them thoroughly under cold running water, to wash away some of those 'unusual saccharides' which Dr Long mentioned. And if you're really worried about digestibility, follow this process by the additional parboiling-and-rinsing: put the pulses (legumes) into a saucepan, cover them with cold water and boil them for 5 minutes, then turn them into a colander and rinse them again under cold running water.

COOKING

Put the pulses (legumes) into a saucepan or casserole and cover them generously with water or stock. Flavourings can be added, but don't put in any salt, as this toughens the outside of the beans and prevents them from cooking properly. For this reason, if you're using vegetable stock for cooking the beans, make sure that it isn't a salty one – if you're not making your own stock, buy low-salt vegetable stock powder or cubes. Acids, such as vinegar and lemon juice, and also tomatoes, have a similar effect on pulses (legumes), so are best added after the initial cooking, although I have found that tomatoes are alright with the quick-cooking pulses (legumes) in small quantities, or if there is plenty of stock to dilute the acid.

Never add bicarbonate of soda (baking soda) to pulses (legumes); while this may be helpful in that it speeds up the cooking time, it is disastrous from the point of view of their flavour and nutritional value.

Pulses (legumes) can be cooked on top of the stove or in the oven. Obviously it is not worth heating the oven specially, but if it's on to cook something else, such as a fruit cake or casserole, it's a good idea to make use of the heat to cook some pulses (legumes), which can simmer away quietly without any fuss towards the bottom of the oven.

PRESSURE COOKING

Use high pressure and cook the pulses for about a third of the time given. As the time pulses (legumes) take to cook can vary, I find, from batch to batch, it's probably best to look at them a little before you think they should be done, to make sure.

Some of the pulses (legumes), particularly the split red lentils and split peas, tend to 'froth up' when they come to the boil, and this can clog the valve of the pressure cooker. To avoid this, just add a couple of tablespoons of oil to the cooking water.

USING A SLOW COOKER (CROCKPOT)

It's best to follow the manufacturer's instructions for this, but basically you just put the pulses (legumes) into the pot and cover them with water – which can be hot or cold – then put the lid on and leave them to cook. The cooking time varies according to the type of pulse (legume), the amount you're using, whether you put them in hot or cold water and the temperature setting. As a rough guide, starting from cold, with the temperature set at high, split red lentils take about 1 hour, butter beans 4–5 hours.

RED KIDNEY BEANS – A WARNING

You may have heard that, under certain conditions, it can be dangerous to eat red kidney beans. The toxic factor is most probably a haemagglutinin which may lead to acute gastroenteritis if not destroyed by adequate cooking. Soaking and rinsing the beans prior to cooking reduces the haemagglutinins by two-thirds to about the level present in other dried beans, soaked or unsoaked. The danger can be eliminated entirely by *ensuring that the beans are allowed to boil vigorously for 10 minutes* before lowering the heat and letting the beans cook gently until tender. It is safe to use a slow cooker (crockpot) *provided the beans are boiled for 10 minutes* as above, before being put into the pot.

STORING COOKED PULSES (LEGUMES)

Cooked pulses (legumes) will keep for several days in a covered container in the fridge and they also freeze well. I find it worthwhile cooking a double batch, using half and storing the rest in either the fridge or freezer, ready for another meal. This saves time, effort and fuel, particularly with the slower cooking pulses (legumes). On the other hand, I think that to keep large stocks of ready cooked beans in the freezer would be somehow to miss the point of them when they keep so well in their dried state.

Incidentally, most of the dishes in this book, including pulse (legume) soups and salads – apart from fresh garnishes like parsley and lettuce leaves, of course – will freeze beautifully after cooking. Except for little croquettes and rissoles, which can be fried from frozen, I find it best to let them thaw out completely before heating.

cooking times

Times given are for soaked beans unless otherwise stated.

ADZUKI BEANS	30 minutes
BLACK BEANS	1 hour
BLACK EYED BEANS (PEAS)	30–45 minutes
BORLOTTI BEANS	1 hour
BRITISH FIELD BEANS	30 minutes
BROAD (FAVA) BEANS	1½ hours
BUTTER BEANS	1¼ hours
CANNELLINI BEANS	1 hour
CHICK PEAS (GARBANZO BEANS)	1½–3 hours
FLAGEOLET BEANS	1 hour
FUL MEDAMES BEANS	1 hour
HARICOT (NAVY) BEANS	1–1½ hours
KIDNEY BEANS	1 hour
LENTILS, GREEN OR BROWN	30–45 minutes
UNSOAKED	1–1¼ hours
LENTILS, PUY	25 minutes
UNSOAKED	40 minutes
LENTILS, SPLIT RED	15–20 minutes
UNSOAKED	20–30 minutes
LIMA BEANS	45–60 minutes
MUNG BEANS	20–30 minutes
UNSOAKED	30–40 minutes
PEAS	45 minutes
PINTO BEANS	1–1¼ hours
SOYA BEANS (SOYBEANS)	3–4 hours
SPLIT PEAS	30 minutes
UNSOAKED	40–45 minutes

soups

Making dried peas, beans and lentils into soup is one of the oldest and most basic of all cooking techniques and one which has produced subsistence food for generations the world over. Almost every country seems to have its pea, bean or lentil soup, from the spicy dal soups of India to the fasolada of Greece, the shurit ads of Egypt and the sopa de panela of Spain.

It is not difficult to make soup from pulses (legumes); in fact I think it's easier than making fresh vegetable soups because the pulses (legumes) need so little preparation. With the exception of the quick-cooking split red lentils, I do think it is worth trying to make time to soak the pulses (legumes) though, because not only does this speed up the cooking time, it also makes them more digestible, as I've explained on page xx.

Although they can be very filling – and some of these soups make a meal in themselves – pulse (legume) soups don't have to be so substantial, because it's easy to vary their character by the amount of liquid you use and how you present them. For instance, it would be hard to get two soups more different from the filling Pistou from the South of France, which you can just about stand a spoon up in, and the thin, elegant Bean and Watercress Soup – yet they both have haricot (navy) beans as their base.

bean and carrot soup

This is a pretty, pale golden soup with a creamy consistency, and the combination of beans and milk is excellent from the protein point of view.

serves 4–5

125g/4oz/heaping ½ cup haricot (navy) beans, soaked, drained and rinsed
900ml/1½ pints/3¾ cups vegetable stock or water
1 large onion, peeled and sliced
1 celery stalk, sliced
2 large carrots, scraped and diced
a bouquet garni – a sprig or two of parsley, a sprig of thyme and a bayleaf, tied together
25g/1oz/2tbsp butter
25g/1oz/3tbsp plain (all-purpose) flour
300ml/10fl oz/1¼ cups milk
sea salt
freshly ground black pepper
grated nutmeg

To serve
chopped fresh parsley

Put the beans into a large saucepan with the stock or water and simmer them gently for 45 minutes, then add the onion, celery, carrots and the bouquet garni. Cook them all for another 30 minutes or so until the beans and vegetables are tender. Remove the bouquet garni and sieve the soup, or whizz it in the food processor or blender.

Melt the butter in a large, clean saucepan and stir in the flour; when it 'froths', remove the saucepan from the heat and stir in the puréed soup. Put the saucepan back on the heat and stir the soup until it has thickened. Leave it to simmer gently for 10–15 minutes to cook the flour, then mix in the milk and season the soup with sea salt, freshly ground black pepper and some grated nutmeg. Reheat the soup, but don't let it boil. Serve it sprinkled with chopped parsley.

butter bean and tomato soup

Served with garlic bread and a salad or some fruit, this hearty soup makes a complete meal.
Lima beans can be used instead of butter beans; they will take 45–60 minutes to cook.

serves 3–4

Soak, drain and rinse the beans as usual. Put them into
a large saucepan with the water or stock and the bayleaf
and simmer them until tender – about 1¹/₄ hours.
Meanwhile, peel and slice the onions and fry them lightly
in the butter until they're soft – about 10 minutes – then
add them to the cooked beans, together with the tomatoes
and some sea salt and freshly ground black pepper.
Bring them up to the boil and simmer gently for about
10 minutes. Check seasoning, adding more sea salt and
freshly ground black pepper and a little sugar if you think
it needs them. Serve sprinkled with parsley. You can whizz
this soup in the food processor or blender if you prefer –
remove the bayleaf first.

225g/8oz/heaping 1 cup
butter beans
900ml/1½ pints/3¾ cups
water or vegetable stock
1 bayleaf
2 large onions
25g/1oz/2tbsp butter
450g/1lb tomatoes, peeled
and chopped – or use
canned ones
sea salt
freshly ground black pepper
a little sugar

To serve
chopped fresh parsley

chilled split green pea soup with mint

If you normally think of pulse (legume) soups as filling cold-weather food, do try this chilled soup. It makes a useful protein-rich first course for the summer and is very refreshing.

serves 4

2tbsp vegetable oil
1 large onion, peeled and chopped
1 celery stalk, chopped
8 sprigs of fresh mint
125g/4oz/½ cup split green peas
1 litre/1¾ pints/1 quart vegetable stock
pinch of ground cloves
1 bayleaf
sea salt
freshly ground black pepper

To serve
a little single (light) cream

Heat the oil in a large saucepan, add the onion and celery and fry them gently, without browning, for 10 minutes.

Meanwhile, remove the leaves from the stems of the mint and put them on one side. Tie the stems together and put them into the saucepan with the onion and celery, split peas, stock, ground cloves and bayleaf. Half cover the saucepan with a lid and simmer gently for about 40 minutes, until the split peas are tender. Remove the bayleaf and mint stems and whizz the soup in the food processor or blender; season it carefully to taste. Put the soup into a bowl and leave it to cool, then chill it.

Taste the soup before serving, because chilling tends to dull the flavour of food. Chop the reserved mint leaves. Spoon the soup into individual bowls and top each portion with a swirl of cream and some chopped mint.

lentil and mushroom soup

The lentils and mushrooms in this soup blend beautifully in flavour and texture. If they don't know, people may think they're just eating mushroom soup, but of course the lentils make it full of nourishment.

serves 4–5

Soak, drain and rinse the lentils as usual. Peel and chop the onion and crush the garlic, then fry them together in the butter in a large saucepan for 5 minutes. Add the mushrooms and fry for a further 4–5 minutes, then add the rinsed and drained lentils and the water or stock. Simmer gently, with a lid on the saucepan, for 1–1¼ hours, or until the lentils are tender. Then whizz the soup in the food processor or blender and season it with sea salt and freshly ground black pepper. Return the soup to the rinsed-out saucepan to reheat it, and serve it sprinkled with the parsley.

125g/4oz/heaping ½ cup green lentils
1 large onion
1 large clove garlic
25g/1oz/2tbsp butter
125g/4oz/1½ cups mushrooms, wiped and chopped
900ml/1½ pints/3¾ cups water or vegetable stock
sea salt
freshly ground black pepper

To serve
2tbsp chopped fresh parsley

lentil and vegetable soup

You can purée this soup if you want to, but personally I prefer not to; it looks attractive with the whole lentils and the colourful pieces of vegetable.

serves 4–5

125g/4oz/heaping ½ cup green lentils
25g/1oz/2tbsp butter
1 onion, peeled and chopped
1 large clove garlic, crushed
2 large carrots, scraped and cut into small dice
2 celery stalks, thinly sliced
2 tomatoes, peeled and chopped
50g/2oz/¾ cup mushrooms, wiped and chopped
75–100g/3–3½oz/about 1½ cups cabbage, washed and chopped
1 litre/1¾ pints/1 quart vegetable stock
a bouquet garni – a couple of sprigs of parsley, a sprig of thyme and a bayleaf, tied together
2tbsp chopped fresh parsley
sea salt
freshly ground black pepper

Soak, drain and rinse the lentils as usual. Melt the butter in a large saucepan and fry the onion for 5 minutes, but don't brown it. Add the garlic and all the other vegetables and cook them very gently for a further 5 minutes, stirring often to prevent sticking. Mix in the rinsed and drained lentils and stir for a minute or two so that the lentils get coated with the butter, then put in the stock and the bouquet garni. Bring the mixture up to the boil, then cover it and leave it to simmer for 1–1¼ hours, or until the lentils are tender. Remove the bunch of herbs; stir in the chopped parsley and some sea salt and freshly ground black pepper to taste. This soup is nice served with grated cheese and some warm, crusty rolls.

cream of butter bean soup

As this soup has a smooth, creamy texture, I like to serve it with some crunchy croûtons of fried bread scattered over the top. Lima beans can be used instead of butter beans; they will take 45–60 minutes to cook.

serves 4–6

Soak, drain and rinse the beans as usual. Peel and chop the onion and potato. Scrape and chop the carrots; trim and slice the celery. Melt the butter in a large saucepan and add the vegetables. Sauté them for 7–8 minutes, but don't let them brown. Add the beans, water or stock, the milk and the bouquet garni. Simmer gently, with a lid half on the saucepan, for about 1¼ hours, or until the beans are tender. Remove the herbs, then whizz the soup in the food processor or blender. Return the soup to the rinsed-out saucepan, stir in the cream and add sea salt, freshly ground black pepper and nutmeg to taste. Reheat the soup, but don't let it boil. Serve each bowl sprinkled with a few croûtons.

125g/4oz/heaping ½ cup butter beans
1 large onion
1 medium-sized potato
2 carrots
2 celery stalks
25g/1oz/2tbsp butter
900ml/1½ pints/3¾ cups water or vegetable stock
300ml/10fl oz/1¼ cups milk
a bouquet garni – a couple of sprigs of parsley, a sprig of thyme and a bayleaf, tied together
4–6tbsp cream
sea salt
freshly ground black pepper
grated nutmeg

To serve
croûtons of fried bread

cream of white bean soup

serves 4–6

225g/8oz/heaping 1 cup
haricot (navy) beans

1 litre/1¾ pints/1 quart
vegetable stock

a bouquet garni – a sprig
each of parsley and thyme
and a bayleaf

1 onion, peeled and chopped

2 cloves garlic, crushed

25g/1oz/2tbsp butter

150ml/5fl oz/⅔ cup single
(light) cream

sea salt

freshly ground black pepper

To serve

2tbsp chopped fresh parsley

Soak, drain and rinse the beans as usual, then put them into a large saucepan with the stock and the bouquet garni. Bring them up to the boil, then simmer them gently, with a lid on the saucepan, for 1–1½ hours, or until the beans are tender. Remove the bouquet garni and whizz the soup in the food processor or blender, or pass it through a food mill. Return the soup to the rinsed-out saucepan.

Fry the onion and garlic in the butter in a small saucepan for about 10 minutes, until the onion is tender but not browned. Stir this onion mixture into the soup, together with the cream and some sea salt and freshly ground black pepper to taste. Reheat the soup, but do not let it boil. Serve it sprinkled with the chopped parsley.

dal soup

One of my favourite soups, this is ideal for serving before a rice and curry meal because the pulse (legume) protein complements the rice, giving first-class nourishment. You can use either split peas or split red lentils.

serves 4–5

Soak, drain and rinse the peas or lentils as usual. Peel and chop the onion and fry it in the oil in a large saucepan for 5 minutes, then add the garlic, turmeric, ginger and bayleaf and fry for a further 5 minutes. Stir in the split peas or lentils and the water. Bring the mixture up to the boil, then let it simmer gently, with a lid on the saucepan, for about 30 minutes, or until the split peas or lentils are soft. Remove the bayleaf and whizz the soup in the food processor or blender, then return the soup to the rinsed-out saucepan.

Wash the lemon, then cut four or five nice circles from it, one to garnish each bowl of soup. Squeeze the rest of the lemon and add enough of the juice to the soup to sharpen it; season carefully with sea salt and freshly ground black pepper. Reheat the soup and serve each bowlful with a circle of lemon floating in it.

175g/6oz/¾ cup yellow split peas or split red lentils
1 large onion
2tbsp oil
1 clove garlic, crushed
1tsp turmeric
1tsp ground ginger
1 bayleaf
1 litre/1¾ pints/1 quart water
1 lemon
sea salt
freshly ground black pepper

fasolada

The most popular way of eating dried beans in Greece is in the form of this soup, sometimes called 'the national dish of Greece', although it is also considered to be rather basic, subsistence food, like pease pudding or baked beans. It's a tasty, warming soup if well made; I do think the olive oil is essential to give the right flavour.

serves 4

6tbsp olive oil
1 large onion, peeled and chopped
2 celery stalks, sliced
2 carrots, scraped and chopped
1 clove garlic, crushed
225g/8oz/heaping 1 cup haricot (navy) beans, soaked, drained and rinsed
1 litre/1¾ pints/1 quart vegetable stock or water
1tbsp tomato paste
2tbsp chopped fresh parsley
sea salt
freshly ground black pepper
a little lemon juice

Heat the oil in a large saucepan and fry the onion, celery, carrots and garlic for 5 minutes, stirring them from time to time to prevent sticking. Then stir in the drained beans, stock or water, tomato paste and parsley and bring the mixture up to the boil. Cover the saucepan with a lid, reduce the heat and simmer gently for 1–1½ hours, or until the beans are tender. Season with sea salt and freshly ground black pepper to taste and a little lemon juice if you think it needs it. This soup can be served as it is, or puréed in the food processor or blender; I think it's nicest when it's been puréed. Wholewheat rolls go well with it and, of course, the wheat complements the bean protein to give good nourishment.

flageolet soup

Creamy and delicate, this soup is equally nice served hot or cold. If serving it cold, use oil, not butter, chill the soup well, and garnish it with extra cream and some chopped chives. The green leek helps to accentuate the natural green colour of the beans.

serves 4

Soak, drain and rinse the beans as usual. Peel and chop the onion. Thoroughly wash and shred the leek, including as much of the green part as possible, then cook the onion and leek gently together in the butter in a good-sized saucepan for about 10 minutes. Add the beans, together with the stock or water, and simmer gently for about 1 hour, or until the beans are tender. Put the soup into the food processor or blender with the cream and parsley and whizz to a smooth, creamy consistency. Season with sea salt and freshly ground black pepper. Return the soup to the rinsed-out saucepan and reheat but do not boil; serve garnished with extra chopped parsley.

125g/4oz/heaping ½ cup flageolet beans
1 small onion
1 leek
25g/1oz/2tbsp butter
900ml/1½ pints/3¾ cups vegetable stock or water
2–4tbsp double (heavy) cream
1tbsp chopped fresh parsley
sea salt
freshly ground black pepper

To serve
a little chopped fresh parsley

bean and watercress soup

The flavour of the fresh watercress comes through quite strongly in this soup, while the beans supply protein.

serves 4–6

175g/6oz/heaping ¾ cup haricot (navy) beans
1 bunch watercress
25g/1oz/2tbsp butter
1 onion, peeled and chopped
1 litre/1¾ pints/1 quart water or vegetable stock
sea salt
freshly ground black pepper

Soak, drain and rinse the beans as usual. Wash the watercress, separating the leaves from the coarse stems; chop the stems. Melt the butter in a large saucepan, add the onion and fry it gently for 5 minutes, without browning, then add the chopped watercress stems and fry for a further few minutes. Mix in the beans and water or stock and bring up to the boil; simmer for 1–1½ hours, or until the beans are tender.

Put the soup and the reserved watercress leaves into the food processor or blender and whizz until smooth. It may be necessary to do this in two batches. Return the soup to the rinsed-out saucepan and reheat; adjust the consistency with a little extra stock if necessary. Season with sea salt and freshly ground black pepper.

lentil soup with curried croûtons

You can vary the thickness of this soup very easily according to the quantity of lentils you use. The amount I've given is right for a rather thin soup – my preference – but for something thicker and more substantial use 175–225g/6–8oz/¾–1 cup lentils.

serves 6

Melt the butter in a large saucepan; add the onion and carrot and fry them together until they're lightly browned. Wash and drain the lentils and mix them in with the onion and carrot. Stir for a minute or two so that all the lentils get coated with the butter, then pour in the stock and add the bayleaf. Bring up to the boil, then turn down the heat and let the mixture simmer gently for about 30 minutes, or until the lentils and vegetables are cooked.

While the soup is cooking, make the croûtons. Remove the crusts from the slices of bread, then cut the bread into 6mm/¹/₄ inch dice. Heat a little oil in a frying pan and add the bread; sprinkle in the curry powder. Turn the pieces of bread in the oil so that they get crisp all over and the curry powder is well distributed. Drain the croûtons on paper towels.

Sieve the soup or whizz it in the food processor or blender after removing the bayleaf. Add enough milk to bring it to a creamy consistency, then mix in the lemon juice and plenty of sea salt and freshly ground black pepper to taste. Return the soup to the rinsed-out saucepan and reheat, but don't let it boil. Serve the soup in individual bowls with a few croûtons on top of each portion.

25g/1oz/2tbsp butter
1 onion, peeled and chopped
1 carrot, scraped and sliced
125g/4oz/heaping ½ cup
split red lentils
900ml/1½ pints/3¾ cups
vegetable stock
1 bayleaf
300ml/10fl oz/1¼ cups milk
2tsp lemon juice
sea salt
freshly ground black pepper

For the croûtons
3 slices of bread
oil for shallow frying
1tsp curry powder

shurit ads

Here's a recipe for lentil soup with garlic and cumin, as it's often served in Egypt. I like the spicy flavour of this soup very much.

serves 4–6

225g/8oz/heaping 1 cup split red lentils
1.2 litres/2 pints/1¼ quarts vegetable stock
1 large onion, peeled and chopped
1 tomato, peeled and sliced
2 large cloves garlic, crushed
25g/1oz/2tbsp butter
1–2tsp ground cumin
sea salt
freshly ground black pepper

Wash and pick over the lentils, then put them into a large saucepan with the stock, half the onion, the tomato and the garlic. Bring up to the boil, then simmer gently for about half an hour, until the lentils are cooked.

Meanwhile, melt the butter in a small saucepan and fry the remaining onion with the cumin until soft and golden.

Whizz the soup in the food processor or blender and return to the rinsed-out saucepan. Reheat and add sea salt and freshly ground black pepper to taste. Serve the soup with the fried onion floating on top as a garnish.

lentil and tomato soup

Although it's generally best to avoid cooking pulses (legumes) with tomatoes, because the acid can prevent them from softening properly, in this recipe the presence of a good quantity of stock and the fact that split red lentils are quick-cooking means that one can get away with it. The result is a lovely tasty soup.

serves 4

Peel and finely chop the onion; slice the celery. Heat the oil in a large saucepan and fry the onion and celery for 7–10 minutes without browning them, then stir in the lentils and mix for a minute or two so that the lentils get coated with the oil. Add the tomatoes and stock or water to the saucepan and bring up to the boil. Half-cover with a lid and simmer gently for 25–30 minutes, by which time the lentils should be cooked. Whizz the soup in the food processor or blender, then return it to the rinsed-out saucepan and season it with sea salt, freshly ground black pepper and lemon juice to taste. Reheat the soup, then serve it garnished with chopped parsley, fresh green against the orange.

1 large onion
1 celery stalk
2tbsp oil
125g/4oz/heaping ½ cup
split red lentils
400g/14oz can tomatoes
900ml/1½ pints/3¾ cups
vegetable stock or water
sea salt
freshly ground black pepper
1–2tbsp lemon juice

To serve
a little chopped fresh
parsley

pistou

Pistou soup came originally from Italy, where it was named after the *pesto* or sauce of pounded basil, oil, pine nuts and cheese with which it was flavoured. When the soup crossed the border into France, *pesto* became *pistou*, and now *pistou* is generally associated with the South of France. Use a good quality bought pesto sauce for this recipe.

serves 6

225g/8oz/heaping 1 cup
haricot (navy) beans
2 onions, peeled and chopped
3tbsp oil
2 carrots, scraped and diced
2 potatoes, peeled and diced
225g/8oz/2 cups courgettes
(zucchini), washed and sliced
125g/4oz/¾ cup French
(fine green) beans, cut into
2.5cm/1 inch pieces
450g/1lb tomatoes, peeled
and chopped
1.75 litres/3 pints/3¾ pints
vegetable stock or water
50g/2oz vermicelli
sea salt
freshly ground black pepper
a little sugar
2–3tbsp pesto

Soak, drain and rinse the beans as usual. Put them into a saucepan, cover with water and cook gently until they're just tender, 1–1½ hours. Drain them, reserving their cooking liquor.

Fry the onions in the oil in a large saucepan for 5–10 minutes, then add all the other vegetables and cook for another 4–5 minutes, stirring often to prevent sticking. Mix in the beans, together with their cooking liquor made up to 1.75 litres/3 pints/3¾ pints with stock or water. Bring the mixture up to the boil, then let it simmer until the vegetables are nearly tender. Put in the vermicelli and cook for about 10 more minutes, until it's done and all the vegetables are fully cooked. Season with sea salt, freshly ground black pepper and perhaps a little sugar.

Mix the pesto into the soup just before serving; check seasoning. It's lovely with lots of grated cheese and hunks of crusty bread.

simple lentil soup

This is my favourite emergency soup. I make it when I find I've suddenly got to produce food for lots of people in the minimum of time. It takes 10–15 minutes with the aid of a pressure cooker, or about 30 minutes without. The butter and garlic are essential to the flavour, but apart from them you can really flavour it up as you like.

serves 4–5

Peel and chop the onion, then fry it in the butter in a large saucepan or pressure cooker pan for 5 minutes. Add the garlic and lentils and stir for a minute, then pour in the stock or water. Bring up to the boil and simmer for 15 minutes or so until the lentils are cooked. Or pressure cook at high pressure for 5 minutes. Whizz the soup in the food processor or blender, then return to the rinsed-out saucepan. Reheat, and add the lemon juice and sea salt and freshly ground black pepper to taste. You can make it thicker, if you prefer, by using 50–125g/ 2–4oz/¼–½ cup more lentils.

1 large onion
25g/1oz/2tbsp butter
1 large clove garlic, crushed
125g/4oz/heaping ½ cup split red lentils
900ml/1½ pints/3¾ cups vegetable stock or water
1tbsp lemon juice
sea salt
freshly ground black pepper

sopa de panela

Chick peas (garbanzo beans) are used a lot in Spanish cookery. In this soup their flavour combines beautifully with mint and garlic.

serves 4

225g/8oz/heaping 1 cup chick peas (garbanzo beans)
2 cloves garlic, crushed
a handful of fresh mint, stems removed
a small handful of fresh parsley, stems removed
6tbsp olive oil
sea salt
freshly ground black pepper
2 slices of bread, crusts removed

Soak, drain and rinse the chick peas (garbanzo beans) as usual, then put them into a saucepan and cover them generously with water. Simmer until they're very tender, then drain them and measure the liquid, making it up to 900ml/1½ pints/3¾ cups with extra water if necessary. Put the chick peas (garbanzo beans), measured liquid, garlic, mint, parsley and half the oil into the food processor or blender and whizz at high speed until smooth. It may be necessary to do this in two batches. Return the soup to the rinsed-out saucepan, season with sea salt and freshly ground black pepper and reheat gently. While this is happening, cut the bread into little cubes and fry in the remaining oil until golden brown. Serve the soup sprinkled with the fried bread croûtons.

spinach and lentil soup

Richly flavoured and satisfying, this is a lovely warming soup to serve on a cold day.

serves 4

Wash the lentils and pick them over carefully, then put them into a bowl, cover them with cold water and leave to soak as usual. Then drain and rinse them. Peel and chop the onion and fry it in the butter in a large saucepan for 10 minutes, until it's soft but not browned. Add the lentils and the garlic and stir them for a minute or two so that they all get coated with the butter, then pour in the stock or water. Bring the mixture up to the boil, then let it simmer gently for about 45 minutes, until the lentils are soft. You can of course use a pressure cooker for this, and in fact I usually do. In this case, fry the onion in the pressure cooker pan and proceed as above, cooking the soup at high pressure for about 15 minutes.

While the lentils are cooking, wash the spinach in several changes of cold water, then chop it roughly. Add the spinach to the cooked lentil mixture, cover and simmer gently for about 10 minutes, until the spinach is soft. Whizz the soup in the food processor or blender, then return it to the rinsed-out saucepan. Reheat, and season with sea salt, freshly ground black pepper and plenty of lemon juice. This soup is very nice as it is, but it's even better if you serve it topped with some crispy fried bread croûtons or a swirl of cream.

125g/4oz/heaping ½ cup green lentils
1 large onion
25g/1oz/2tbsp butter
1 large clove garlic, crushed
1 litre/1¾ pints/1 quart vegetable stock or water
225g/8oz spinach
sea salt
freshly ground black pepper
2–3tsp lemon juice

To serve
croûtons or a little single (light) cream

first courses, salads, pâtés and spreads

I know that most people think of beans and lentils in terms of hot, often filling, dishes, but perhaps surprisingly, I think they are possibly at their best when served cold as a first course or part of a salad. Few dishes are more delicious, in my opinion, than a smooth, well-made chick pea hummus, all creamy beige, garnished with pale green olive oil, yellow lemon wedges and a flush of red paprika; and, on a hot summer's day, chilled haricot (navy) bean salad, glistening with vinaigrette dressing and fragrant with fresh green herbs, is always a treat. And if you're trying to economize, these bean and lentil salads and first courses are useful because they provide good protein cheaply, and the rest of the meal can contain that much less – a colourful rice and vegetable mixture, for instance, or vegetables in a light, cheesy sauce.

The important thing to remember when serving pulses (legumes) chilled is that they must be really well cooked. Not soggy, but certainly very tender, because chilling them firms them up and if they're a little on the underdone side it can make them seem a bit hard. Also, as chilling food tends to dull the flavour, make sure that the mixture is well seasoned. For this reason, it's well worth using a really good quality olive oil when possible – and lovely fresh green herbs in the summer.

aïgroissade

Strictly speaking this Provençal salad consists of tender young vegetables and chick peas (garbanzo beans), cooked and cooled and mixed with aïoli, that special garlic dressing which is like mayonnaise. I tend to cheat a bit by simply adding crushed garlic to some good-quality bottled mayonnaise, and I generally use a mixture of half mayonnaise and half plain yogurt, as in this recipe, as it's lighter and less fattening.

serves 3–4

Soak, drain, rinse and cook the chick peas (garbanzo beans) as usual; drain them well. Scrape the potatoes and carrots and cook them in boiling salted water until they're nearly tender. Wash the shelled broad (fava) beans and top and tail the French (fine green) beans, then add them to the pan of potatoes and carrots. When all the vegetables are tender, drain and cool them, then cut them into even-sized pieces. Drain and slice the artichoke hearts and mix them with the other vegetables, together with the chick peas (garbanzo beans). Mix together the garlic, mayonnaise and yogurt, add salt and pepper to taste, then add the vegetables, turning them gently so that they are all coated with the creamy mayonnaise mixture. Serve sprinkled with chopped parsley. This is very nice with warm wholewheat rolls.

125g/4oz/½ heaping cup chick peas (garbanzo beans),
225g/8oz new potatoes
125g/4oz new carrots
sea salt
125g/4oz/heaping ½ cup shelled broad (fava) beans
125g/4oz French (fine green) beans
400g/14oz can artichoke hearts
1 large clove garlic, crushed, or more according to taste
6 good tbsp mayonnaise
6 good tbsp plain yogurt
freshly ground black pepper

To serve
chopped fresh parsley

beany salad bowl

You can use any type of bean for this salad, such as chick peas (garbanzo beans) or butter or lima beans, or some of the more unusual ones.

serves 4

6tbsp olive oil
2tbsp wine vinegar
½tsp dry mustard
1tsp sugar
sea salt
freshly ground black pepper
125g/4oz/½ cup beans, soaked and cooked until tender, then drained
2tbsp chopped fresh green herbs
1 celery heart, chopped
1 sweet green pepper, deseeded and sliced
2 large carrots, scraped and coarsely grated
10cm/4 inch cucumber, diced
1 sweet apple, diced

Into a salad bowl put the oil, vinegar, mustard, sugar, some sea salt and a good grinding of black pepper. Give it a good stir, so that it's all blended, then add the beans, green herbs and the rest of the ingredients. Mix well so that everything gets coated with the dressing. It's nice served with homemade wholewheat bread and unsalted butter, and of course the wheat protein complements the bean protein to give excellent nourishment.

bean, apple and beetroot salad

serves 2–4

Soak, drain, rinse and cook the beans as usual; drain them well. Make a dressing by mixing together the honey, oil, vinegar and some sea salt and freshly ground black pepper and pour this over the butter beans, turning them gently in it. Peel and dice the beetroot (beet); wash, core and slice the apples. Add them to the beans and mix gently, then chill the salad. Serve it garnished with chopped fresh mint.

125g/4oz/heaping ½ cup
butter or lima beans
1tsp honey
3tbsp oil
1tbsp red wine vinegar
sea salt
freshly ground black pepper
1 large cooked beetroot
(beet)
2 sweet apples

To serve
a little chopped fresh mint

beans and mushrooms with coriander

This is one of my favourite bean salads, succulent and spicy. It makes an excellent first course. Serve it with soft rolls to mop up the delicious juices.

serves 4 as a first course, 2 as a main salad dish

125g/4oz/heaping ½ cup butter or lima beans
225g/8oz/3 cups small white button mushrooms
8tbsp vegetable oil
3–4tsp ground coriander
2 cloves garlic, crushed
juice of 1 lemon
sea salt
freshly ground black pepper

To serve
crisp lettuce leaves
chopped fresh parsley

Soak, drain and rinse the beans as usual. Cover them with fresh water, simmer them gently until they're tender, then drain them. Wash the mushrooms and halve or quarter them if necessary. Heat the oil in a saucepan and add the mushrooms and coriander. Fry the mushrooms for 1–2 minutes, just to tenderize them, but don't let them get soggy. Remove the pan from the heat and add the beans, garlic and lemon juice. Mix gently, adding sea salt and freshly ground black pepper to taste. Let the mixture cool, then chill it, and serve it on a base of crisp lettuce, garnished with chopped parsley.

bean, tomato and onion salad

serves 2–3

Put the garlic, oil, vinegar and some sea salt and freshly ground black pepper into a bowl. Mix them well together, then stir in the beans, being careful not to mash them, and the onion, tomatoes and olives. Turn them gently in the dressing until they're all shiny and delicious-looking. Chill the mixture before serving. Fresh basil is lovely chopped over the top of this salad.

1 clove garlic, crushed
3tbsp oil
1tbsp wine vinegar
sea salt
freshly ground black pepper
125g/4oz/heaping ½ cup
butter or lima beans,
soaked, cooked and drained
1 onion, peeled and sliced
into rings
3 firm tomatoes, sliced
a few black olives, if
available

cabbage and bean salad

serves 4

1tbsp wine vinegar
3tbsp salad oil
1tsp sugar
½tsp dry mustard
sea salt
freshly ground black pepper
1tbsp chopped fresh herbs
350g/12oz/6 cups white cabbage, finely shredded
2 celery stalks, chopped
½ sweet green pepper, deseeded and chopped
2 carrots, grated
2–3tbsp sultanas (golden raisins), washed and drained
125g/4oz/½ cup dried beans – any firm type – soaked, cooked and drained

Put the vinegar, oil, sugar, mustard and some sea salt and freshly ground black pepper into a bowl and mix them together. Add all the other ingredients and stir them gently, so that they all get coated with the dressing. This is nice served with wholewheat rolls and some curd or cottage cheese.

cannellini, apple and celery salad

You could use any white beans for this salad, but cannellini are especially nice because of their size and shape.

serves 2–3

Soak, drain, rinse and cook the beans as usual; drain. Mix together the oil and lemon juice and some sea salt and freshly ground black pepper and add this to the beans, mixing gently. Wash and slice the celery. Wash the apples and peel them if the skin is tough, then cut them into dice, discarding the core. Add the celery and apples to the beans, along with the raisins. Turn the salad gently with a spoon before serving so that everything gets mixed together and coated with the dressing.

125g/4oz/heaping ½ cup cannellini beans
3tbsp oil
1tbsp lemon juice
sea salt
freshly ground black pepper
1 celery heart
2 sweet apples
2tbsp raisins, washed and drained

chick pea, apple and leek salad

serves 3

125g/4oz/heaping ½ cup chick peas (garbanzo beans)
2 sweet apples
1tbsp lemon juice
1tbsp oil
1 medium-sized leek
1 tomato
sea salt
freshly ground black pepper

To serve
crisp lettuce leaves

Soak, drain, rinse and cook the chick peas (garbanzo beans) as usual, then drain them. Wash the apples and peel them if they look as if they need it, then cut them into smallish dice, discarding the cores. Add the apples to the chick peas (garbanzo beans), together with the lemon juice and oil. Wash the leek carefully, then cut it into thin rings, using the white part and as much of the green as possible; dice the tomato. Add the leek and tomato to the chick pea (garbanzo bean) mixture. Season with sea salt and freshly ground black pepper. Serve the salad on a base of crisp lettuce leaves.

chick pea nibbles

These puffy, garlic-flavoured chick peas (garbanzo beans) always seem to go down well with drinks, but you can also serve them as the protein part of a light meal, accompanied by a dollop of mayonnaise, some sliced lemon and a crisp salad, in which case the quantity I've given would probably serve two people.

serves 2–4

Soak, drain, rinse and cook the chick peas (garbanzo beans) as usual. Mix together the flour and garlic; season with sea salt and freshly ground black pepper. Toss the chick peas (garbanzo beans) in the seasoned flour, coating them as well as you can. Heat the butter and oil in a frying pan and add the chick peas (garbanzo beans); sprinkle any remaining flour on top of them. Gently fry the chick peas (garbanzo beans), turning them frequently, until they're crisp and golden all over. Drain on paper towels and serve immediately, while they're all crisp and light.

125g/4oz/heaping ½ cup
chick peas (garbanzo beans)
4tbsp wholewheat
self-raising flour
1 clove garlic, crushed
sea salt
freshly ground black pepper
25g/1oz/2tbsp butter
2tbsp oil

chick pea salad

This Middle Eastern salad is good with crisp lettuce leaves and chilled plain yogurt.

serves 4

175g/6oz/scant 1 cup chick peas (garbanzo beans)
2 cloves garlic
2tbsp olive oil
2tbsp lemon juice
sea salt
freshly ground black pepper
1 small onion, peeled and sliced into rings
3tbsp chopped fresh parsley

Cover the chick peas (garbanzo beans) with plenty of cold water and leave them to soak overnight. Then drain them and rinse thoroughly under cold water. Cook the chick peas (garbanzo beans) gently in fresh cold water until they're tender, then drain them thoroughly. Meanwhile, peel and crush the garlic, put it into a medium-sized bowl and mix in the olive oil, lemon juice and some sea salt and freshly ground black pepper. Add the drained chick peas (garbanzo beans), which can still be hot, and turn them in the dressing. Add the onion and parsley and leave to get cold. Check seasoning; serve cold or chilled.

chick pea and spinach salad with yogurt

There's a lovely contrast of texture and colour in this Middle Eastern salad: firm chick peas (garbanzo beans) against soft, bright green spinach and smooth, creamy white yogurt.

serves 4–6 as a first course, 2–3 as a salad meal

Thoroughly wash the spinach. Cook it without extra water until it's tender, then cool, drain and chop it. Add the chick peas (garbanzo beans) to the cooled spinach, together with the olive oil, vinegar and a good seasoning of sea salt and freshly ground black pepper. Mix well together, being careful not to break up the chick peas (garbanzo beans), then chill the salad until required.

To serve, arrange the spinach and chick pea (garbanzo bean) mixture on a plate and spoon the yogurt on top. Sprinkle with chopped parsley. Some thin buttered brown bread goes well with this.

If you want a crunchier texture, try adding some raw onion rings to the salad mixture; it's also nice with a flavouring of crushed garlic.

450g/1lb spinach

175g/6oz/scant 1 cup chick peas (garbanzo beans), cooked and drained

6tbsp olive oil

2tbsp wine vinegar

sea salt

freshly ground black pepper

150ml/5fl oz/⅔ cup plain yogurt

1–2tbsp chopped fresh parsley

lentil and mushroom pâté

This curiously pleasant mixture can be served as part of a salad, piled on crisp lettuce leaves, sprinkled with a little olive oil and some onion rings and surrounded by wedges of hardboiled egg. Or, in smaller portions on individual dishes, it makes a delicious first course. Alternatively, it can be served in a pâté dish, with Melba toast and butter, or thin brown bread and butter. It also makes a good sandwich filling, with or without the addition of thin slices of crisp raw onion or cucumber, tomato or other salad ingredients. Altogether rather a useful mixture, and not difficult to make, although I usually try to cook the lentils with another batch – or cook more and save the rest for something else – because it seems rather a small quantity to cook on its own.

serves 2 as a salad meal, 4–6 as a first course, pâté or sandwich filling

125g/4oz/heaping ½ cup green lentils
50g/2oz/¾ cup button mushrooms
1 clove garlic
40g/1½oz/3tbsp butter
1tbsp chopped fresh parsley
sea salt
freshly ground black pepper
2–4tsp lemon juice

Soak, drain, rinse and cook the lentils as usual, until very tender and beginning to disintegrate. Drain off any extra liquid – it won't be needed for this recipe, but keep it for a gravy or soup or something because it's full of flavour and nourishment. Wipe the mushrooms and chop them up fairly finely; crush the garlic. Melt the butter in a small saucepan and fry the mushrooms and garlic for 2–3 minutes, then remove them from the heat and mix in the lentils and parsley. Season with sea salt, freshly ground black pepper and lemon juice. Chill before using.

mediterranean lentil salad

This popular salad is one of the simplest, but also one of the best. It's lovely on a hot day, served really cold, with a crisp lettuce salad and an iced drink.

serves 4

Soak the lentils for a couple of hours or so in cold water, then drain and rinse them and cook gently in fresh cold water until they're tender. Drain the lentils well. Add to the hot lentils as much olive oil as they will take, then season the mixture with sea salt and freshly ground black pepper, and cool and chill it. Just before serving, mix in the onion rings. Garnish with the wedges of egg and the lemon slices, and hand round extra olive oil and thin slices of brown bread and butter.

225g/8oz/heaping 1 cup green lentils
olive oil
sea salt
freshly ground black pepper
1 onion, peeled and sliced into rings

To serve
hardboiled egg wedges
lemon slices

creamy bean dip

This is nice with a crisp salad or garlic bread; it's also good with sliced tomato and onion as a sandwich filling.

serves 2 as a salad, 4 as a first course

125g/4oz/heaping ½ cup butter or lima beans
1 clove garlic, crushed
1tbsp olive oil
sea salt
freshly ground black pepper

To serve
paprika
black olives

Soak, drain and rinse the beans as usual, then cook them in fresh water until they're very tender; drain. Mash the beans thoroughly with a fork or, if you want a really smooth texture, whizz them in the food processor or blender or pass them through a food mill. Beat the garlic and oil into the beans and add sea salt and freshly ground black pepper to taste. Chill.

I think this looks attractive served forked up into a cone shape on a flat plate, sprinkled with paprika and garnished with a few black olives. Some crisp lettuce leaves and watercress sprigs tucked round the edge look nice too, and really turn it into a light meal.

curried lentil and pineapple salad

serves 4

Fry the garlic and onion in half the oil in a medium-sized saucepan for 5 minutes, then add the curry powder and the washed and drained lentils. Fry for a further 4–5 minutes, stirring often to prevent sticking. Mix in the water and let the mixture cook very gently for 20–30 minutes, after which the lentils should be tender in texture, beige-gold in colour and all the water absorbed. Remove the saucepan from the heat and add the pineapple, green pepper, vinegar, remaining oil, and sea salt and black pepper to taste. Cool, then chill. Serve the salad piled up on lettuce leaves and garnished with slices of tomato and raw onion rings. Alternatively, it's very nice served scattered with desiccated (dried shredded) coconut and garnished with sliced banana rings, which have first been tossed in a little lemon juice to prevent them from discolouring.

2 cloves garlic, crushed
1 medium-sized onion, peeled and chopped
6tbsp oil
1tbsp curry powder
225g/8oz/heaping 1 cup split red lentils
300ml/10fl oz/1¼ cups water
400g/14oz can pineapple pieces, drained and chopped
1 small sweet green pepper, deseeded and chopped
1tbsp wine vinegar
sea salt
freshly ground black pepper

To serve
lettuce leaves
slices of tomato
a few onion rings

curried lentil spread

This is a good mixture for sandwiches or little savoury biscuits or crackers.

serves 2–4

125g/4oz/heaping ½ cup split red lentils
200ml/7fl oz/scant 1 cup water
1 small onion, peeled and finely chopped
25g/1oz/2tbsp butter
2tsp curry powder
sea salt
freshly ground black pepper

Wash the lentils and cook them in the water for 20–30 minutes, until they're tender and have absorbed all the water. Mash them roughly with a fork. Fry the onion in the butter until it's tender, then add the curry powder and fry for another 1–2 minutes. Blend this mixture into the cooked lentils to make a fairly smooth paste, then season to taste and leave the spread to get cold before using it.

flageolet and avocado salad

I'm particularly fond of this salad because its colours are so pleasing: pale green flageolet beans, yellow-green avocado and lettuce, dark green chives. It also tastes very good.

serves 2 as a salad meal, 4 as a first course

Soak, drain, rinse and cook the beans as usual, then drain and cool them. Mix the oil with the vinegar, mustard and some sea salt and freshly ground black pepper, and add to the beans. Halve the avocado and gently remove the skin and the stone, then slice the flesh and add it to the beans. Turn the mixture gently, so that everything gets coated with the dressing, then serve it spooned on top of the lettuce leaves and sprinkled with the chopped chives.

125g/4oz/heaping ½ cup flageolet beans
3tbsp oil
1tbsp white wine vinegar
¼tsp dry mustard
sea salt
freshly ground black pepper
1 ripe avocado
a few crisp lettuce leaves
2tbsp chopped fresh chives

flageolet and button mushroom salad

serves 2 as a salad,
4 as a first course

1 clove garlic, crushed
3tbsp oil
1tbsp lemon juice
sea salt
freshly ground black pepper
125g/4oz/heaping ½ cup
flageolet beans, soaked,
cooked, drained and cooled
175g/6oz/2¼ cups very
fresh white button
mushrooms
1tbsp chopped fresh parsley

First of all make a dressing by mixing together the garlic, oil, lemon juice and some sea salt and freshly ground black pepper. Pour this dressing over the beans and mix them well, so that they're all coated with it. Wash the mushrooms, then slice them fairly finely and stir them into the bean mixture, together with the chopped parsley. Check the seasoning, then chill the salad.

flageolet and onion salad

**serves 2 as a salad,
4 as a first course**

Soak, drain, rinse and cook the beans as usual, then drain them well. Mix together the lemon juice, olive oil and a seasoning of sea salt and freshly ground black pepper. Pour this dressing over the beans – you can do this while they're still warm or you can use cold beans. Add the onions and stir the mixture so that everything is well mixed. Cool the salad if necessary; serve it chilled and spooned over crisp lettuce leaves.

125g/4oz/heaping ½ cup
flageolet beans
1tbsp lemon juice
3tbsp olive oil
sea salt
freshly ground black pepper
6–8 large spring (green)
onions, washed, trimmed
and sliced

To serve
crisp lettuce leaves

bean and garlic spread

This makes a pleasant sandwich filling and is also good on little cocktail biscuits or crackers, decorated with small pieces of olive, etc. The basic mixture can be varied in a number of ways.

serves 2–4

125g/4oz/heaping ½ cup haricot (navy) beans, cooked until tender, then cooled
25g/1oz/2tbsp soft butter
1 clove garlic, crushed
a few drops of lemon juice
sea salt
freshly ground black pepper

Mash the beans to a smooth paste with a fork, then gradually blend in the butter, garlic and lemon juice. Season the spread well with sea salt and freshly ground black pepper.

variations

bean and parsley spread

Omit garlic from the recipe and add instead 2tbsp chopped fresh parsley.

bean and fresh herb spread

Instead of the garlic, add 2tbsp chopped fresh herbs: parsley, chives, tarragon, mint, fennel or lovage, whatever is available.

bean and olive spread

Make as above, leaving out the garlic and using instead 4–6 black olives, stoned (pitted) and mashed to a paste.

bean and herb salad

You can use any fresh green herbs for this salad: parsley and chives, of course, and any others available – mint, lovage, tarragon, basil, lemon balm, fennel and dill are all good.

serves 4–6 as a first course, 3–4 as a salad meal

Soak, drain, rinse and cook the beans as usual, then drain them. Mix up a dressing using the vinegar, oil, sea salt, freshly ground black pepper and mustard. Pour this over the beans – you can do this while the beans are still warm. Add the green herbs and mix well. Leave to cool, stirring the mixture from time to time so that all the flavours blend well together. Serve nice and cold.

225g/8oz/heaping 1 cup
haricot (navy) beans
1tbsp wine vinegar
3tbsp oil
sea salt
freshly ground black pepper
¼tsp mustard
2–3tbsp chopped fresh
green herbs

greek bean salad

This is a deliciously rich-tasting bean salad and is good with warm crusty rolls and a bowl of crisp lettuce and watercress.

serves 4

225g/8oz/heaping 1 cup haricot (navy) beans
8tbsp olive oil – or half olive, half vegetable oil
2 cloves garlic, crushed
1tsp sea salt
2tsp tomato paste
2 sprigs thyme
1 bayleaf
150ml/5fl oz/⅔ cup water
juice of 1 lemon
1 onion, peeled
freshly ground black pepper

To serve
chopped fresh parsley

Soak, drain and rinse the beans, then cook them in plenty of water until nearly tender; drain. Heat the oil in a good-sized saucepan, add the beans and cook them very gently for about 10 minutes. Stir in the garlic, sea salt, tomato paste, thyme, bayleaf and water – you can use some of the water in which the beans were cooked – and simmer gently, without a lid, until the liquid has reduced to a thick, terracotta-coloured sauce and the beans are tender. Cool, then add the lemon juice and the onion, sliced into thin rounds. Season with more sea salt and freshly ground black pepper if necessary. Chill the salad and serve it sprinkled with chopped parsley.

hummus

Eaten throughout the Middle East, this creamy dip is, in my opinion, one of the best pulse (legume) dishes. It's useful as part of a salad meal, as a spread or dip, as a sandwich filling or unusual first course. It's extremely rich in protein and calcium.

serves 4 as a first course, 2 as a salad meal

Soak, rinse and drain the chick peas (garbanzo beans), then cook them until they're tender. Drain them, reserving the cooking water. Put the chick peas (garbanzo beans) into the food processor or blender, together with 4–5tbsp of the cooking water, the garlic, lemon juice, tahini and half the olive oil. Whizz until smooth, adding a little more cooking water to thin the mixture if necessary. Season carefully with sea salt. Chill the mixture.

To serve the hummus, spoon it on to a flat dish and smooth it, then fork over the top. Pour the remaining olive oil gently over the hummus, sprinkle with paprika and garnish with lemon wedges.

125g/4oz/heaping ½ cup chick peas (garbanzo beans)
1–2 cloves garlic, crushed
2tbsp lemon juice
2tbsp tahini paste
4tbsp olive oil
sea salt

To serve
paprika
lemon wedges

lentil and tomato spread

This is nice in sandwiches with some raw onion, chutney or sliced tomato.

serves 2–4

125g/4oz/heaping ½ cup split red lentils
200ml/7fl oz/scant 1 cup water
25g/1oz/2tbsp softened butter
1tbsp tomato paste
a few drops of lemon juice
sea salt
freshly ground black pepper

Cook the lentils in the water for 20–30 minutes, until they're tender and there's no water left, then let them cool. Mash the butter, tomato paste, a few drops of lemon juice and some sea salt and freshly ground black pepper into the cooked lentils to make a smoothish paste.

variation

lentil and chive spread

Make this as above but leave out the tomato paste and add 1–2tbsp chopped fresh chives instead.

red bean and orange salad

A salad for a grey winter's day because the vivid colour is such a tonic. It's useful when conventional salad vegetables are not at their best.

serves 4

Soak, drain and rinse the kidney beans as usual, then put them into a saucepan with plenty of cold water. Boil the beans vigorously for 10 minutes, then lower the heat and cook gently for about 1 hour, or until they're tender. Drain and cool them.

Wash and slice the celery; cut the peel and pith from the oranges and slice the fruit into thin rounds. Mix together the orange, celery, beans, oil and mint. Add sea salt and freshly ground black pepper to taste. Chill before serving.

175g/6oz/1 cup red kidney beans
1 celery heart
4 large oranges
2tbsp oil
2tbsp chopped fresh mint
sea salt
freshly ground black pepper

red bean salad

Simple and well known, but still one of the best bean salads. Here's my version, which goes well with a bowl of lettuce and watercress.

serves 3–4

175g/6oz/1 cup red kidney beans
1 onion
1 clove garlic
1tbsp red wine vinegar
3tbsp olive oil
¼tsp dry mustard
½tsp sugar
1tbsp tomato paste
sea salt
freshly ground black pepper

Soak, drain and rinse the kidney beans as usual, then put them into a saucepan with plenty of cold water. Boil vigorously for 10 minutes, then lower the heat and cook gently for about 1 hour, or until they're tender. Drain.

Peel and slice the onion and crush the garlic. Add the onion and garlic to the beans. Mix together the vinegar, oil, mustard, sugar, tomato paste and some sea salt and freshly ground black pepper. Pour this over the bean mixture, stirring well. As with most bean salads, I think this is better served very cold, and it's worth making it in advance so that the flavours have time to blend.

rice and bean salad

You can use any beans for this salad, though I generally use red kidney beans because their bright colour makes the mixture look so attractive.

serves 4–6

Soak, drain and rinse the kidney beans as usual, then put them into a saucepan with plenty of cold water. Boil vigorously for 10 minutes, then lower the heat and cook gently for about 1 hour, or until they're tender.

Wash and pick over the rice, then put it into a saucepan with the water and 1tsp sea salt. Bring it up to the boil and cook it as usual, over a very gentle heat with the lid on the saucepan, until it's just tender and all the water has been absorbed – 45 minutes.

Wash the aubergine (eggplant) and cut it into small pieces. Crush the garlic; peel and chop the onion. Fry the garlic and onion in the oil in a good-sized saucepan for 10 minutes, then add the prepared aubergine (eggplant) and cook for a minute or two longer while you deseed and chop the red pepper and wash and slice the mushrooms. Then add the pepper and mushrooms to the saucepan, also the canned tomatoes, and let everything cook for a further 10 minutes or so.

Using a fork, mix together the cooked rice, the vegetables and the beans; season with sea salt, freshly ground black pepper and Tabasco. Let the salad get quite cold and serve it sprinkled with chopped parsley.

125g/4oz/⅔ cup red kidney beans
225g/8oz/heaping 1 cup long grain brown rice
400ml/14fl oz/1¾ cups water
sea salt
1 medium-sized aubergine (eggplant), weighing about 225g/8oz
1 clove garlic
1 large onion
2tbsp oil
1 sweet red pepper
125g/4oz/1½ cups mushrooms
225g/8oz/1 cup canned tomatoes
freshly ground black pepper
2 drops of Tabasco

To serve
a little chopped fresh parsley

russian red beans with damson sauce

This Russian dish has an unusual sweet flavour which goes well with a crunchy salad of white cabbage.

serves 4–6

225g/8oz/1⅓ cups red kidney beans
2tbsp damson or plum jam
½tsp red wine vinegar
1 clove garlic, crushed
sea salt
½tsp dried basil
½tsp ground coriander

Soak, drain and rinse the kidney beans as usual, then put them into a saucepan with plenty of cold water. Boil vigorously for 10 minutes, the lower the heat and cook gently for about 1 hour, or until they're tender. Drain.

Sieve the jam and put it into a small saucepan with the vinegar. Cook them gently over a low heat until the jam has melted, then add the crushed garlic, a little sea salt and the basil and coriander. Remove from the heat and add to the beans, stirring well so that all the beans get coated. Leave the beans for 2–3 hours, so that the flavours can blend, then serve them very cold.

three bean salad

This colourful salad is good served with hot rolls or garlic bread and another salad of fresh vegetables, such as tomatoes with onion, or lettuce and watercress. The chick peas (garbanzo beans) and haricot (navy) beans can be cooked together, but it is best to cook the red beans separately or you will end up with a whole pan of pink beans. Other beans can be used, but choose ones which will keep their shape after cooking.

serves 4

Soak the beans in separate bowls, then drain and rinse them. Cook the red kidney beans in one saucepan (boiling them vigorously for the first 10 minutes) and the chick peas (garbanzo beans) and haricot (navy) beans together in another, with plenty of water, until they're tender. Drain.

Put the mustard and sugar in a bowl, blend with a little of the vinegar, then add the rest of the vinegar and the oil. Pour this dressing over the beans – this can be done while they're still hot – and mix well, being careful not to break them up. Add the herbs and sea salt and freshly ground black pepper to taste and leave to get cold. Serve chilled.

75g/3oz/½ cup red kidney beans
75g/3oz/scant ½ cup chick peas (garbanzo beans)
75g/3oz/scant ½ cup haricot (navy) beans
½tsp dry mustard
½tsp caster sugar
2tbsp wine vinegar
6tbsp olive oil
2–3tbsp chopped fresh green herbs – parsley, mint, chives, tarragon, fennel – whatever is available
sea salt
freshly ground black pepper

bakes and casseroles

The recipes in this section range from thrifty dishes such as lentil toad-in-the-hole, to the exotic Middle Eastern musakka'a, a colourful mixture of aubergines (eggplants), sweet peppers, tomatoes and chick peas (garbanzo beans), and a spicy red bean moussaka. There's also an easy lentil and spinach casserole and lentils with fennel and shepherds' beany pie, as well as Boston baked beans.

baked butter beans and cheese

Although this dish takes about 2 hours to cook, the actual preparation is quick and easy, and while it's cooking you can really forget about it. Lima beans can be used instead of butter beans; they will take 45–60 minutes to cook at the beginning of the recipe.

serves 4

Soak the beans as usual, then drain and rinse them. Fry the onion, garlic, carrots and celery in the butter in a large, heavy-based saucepan for 10 minutes, then stir in the beans and add the bouquet garni and enough stock to cover by about 1cm/½ inch. Bring the mixture up to the boil, then put a lid on the saucepan, turn the heat down and leave to simmer very gently for about 1¼ hours, until the beans are tender. Check the level of the liquid from time to time and add more stock if necessary.

Preheat the oven to 190°C/375°F/Gas 5. Remove the bouquet garni from the cooked beans and add to the saucepan the tomatoes and chopped parsley; season with sea salt, freshly ground black pepper and a little chilli powder. Turn the mixture into a greased ovenproof dish and sprinkle with grated cheese and crumbs. Bake in the oven for about 30 minutes, until golden and crisp on top. This is lovely served with just a simply cooked green vegetable, and perhaps some potatoes too if you're catering for very hungry people.

350g/12oz/1¾ cups butter beans
1 onion, peeled and sliced
1 clove garlic, crushed
2 carrots, sliced
2 celery stalks, sliced
50g/2oz/¼ cup butter
bouquet garni – a sprig each of parsley and thyme, and a bayleaf, tied together
vegetable stock
225g/8oz/1 cup canned tomatoes
2tbsp chopped fresh parsley
sea salt
freshly ground black pepper
chilli powder

For the topping
125g/4oz/1 cup grated cheese
dry crumbs

black eyed bean bake

A simple dish, and one that's popular with children, I find. A nice spicy tomato sauce goes well with it, or a tasty gravy.

350g/12oz/2 cups black eyed beans (peas), soaked in plenty of water overnight
2 large onions, peeled and sliced
3 cloves garlic, crushed
3tbsp vegetable oil
½tsp dried thyme
1tsp dried marjoram
400ml/14fl oz/1¾ cups water or vegetable stock
sea salt
freshly ground black pepper

For the topping
wholewheat breadcrumbs
50g/2oz/½ cup grated cheese

Drain and rinse the beans (peas). Fry the onion and garlic in the oil for 10 minutes, until the onion is tender, then add the beans (peas), herbs and water or stock. Simmer gently, until the beans (peas) are tender, about 30–45 minutes. Preheat the oven to 180°C/350°F/Gas 4. Whizz the bean mixture in a food processor or blender or pass it through a food mill, then season it to taste with sea salt and freshly ground black pepper. Spoon it into a greased, shallow ovenproof dish, then sprinkle it with the wholewheat breadcrumbs and grated cheese. Bake in the oven for about 30 minutes, until the top is golden and crunchy.

boston baked beans

'Boston runs to brains as well as beans and brown bread,' noted William Cowper Brann in *The Iconoclast, Beans and Blood*. Well, here's a recipe for the beans.

serves 4

Soak, drain and rinse the beans as usual, then cook them in fresh water until almost tender; drain them again.

Set the oven to 140°C/275°F/Gas 1. Peel and slice the onion. Heat the oil in a flameproof casserole and fry the onion for about 5 minutes, then add the rest of the ingredients and bring the mixture up to the boil. Cover the casserole and put it into the oven; cook for about 4 hours, stirring occasionally. These beans are lovely served with hot wholewheat bread, or garlic bread.

350g/12oz/1¾ cups haricot (navy) beans
1 large onion
2tbsp oil
1tsp dry mustard
2tsp black treacle (molasses)
150ml/5fl oz/⅔ cup tomato juice – you can use the liquid from a can of tomatoes
2tbsp tomato paste
2tsp brown sugar
300ml/10fl oz/1¼ cups vegetable stock

lentil toad-in-the-hole

With gravy, potatoes and vegetables, this makes a good cheap family meal.

serves 4–6

125g/4oz/heaping ½ cup green lentils

4tbsp oil

1 onion, peeled and chopped

1 clove garlic, crushed

125g/4oz/1 cup mushrooms, wiped and sliced

1tsp dried thyme

sea salt

freshly ground black pepper

For the batter

125g/4oz/¾ cup + 2tbsp self-raising wholewheat flour

½tsp sea salt

2 eggs

300ml/10fl oz/1¼ cups milk

Soak, drain, rinse and cook the lentils as usual, then drain them.

Preheat the oven to 220°C/425°F/Gas 7. Heat 2tbsp of the oil in a good-sized saucepan and fry the onion and garlic for 5 minutes, letting them brown lightly, then add the mushrooms and fry for another 5 minutes. Stir in the lentils and thyme, then sea salt and freshly ground black pepper to season; keep the mixture hot.

Put the remaining oil into a shallow baking pan in which you are going to cook the toad-in-the-hole, and heat in the oven.

Next, make the batter. Sift the flour and sea salt into a bowl and tip in the residue of bran left in the sieve (strainer). Make a well in the middle and add the eggs and about a third of the milk. Beat vigorously with a wooden spoon, gradually incorporating the rest of the milk; beat well.

Pour the batter straight into the sizzling hot fat, then quickly spoon the lentil mixture on top. Bake in the oven for 20–25 minutes, until risen and golden.

fennel and lentil au gratin

This is one of my favourite pulse (legume) dishes; the flavour and texture of the fennel go really well with the lentils.

serves 3–4

Fry the onion in 25g/1oz/2tbsp of the butter in a medium-sized saucepan for 5 minutes, then add the washed lentils and the water or stock and bayleaf. Simmer them gently for 20–30 minutes, until the lentils are soft and golden-beige. Then remove the bayleaf and whizz the lentil mixture in the food processor or blender, adding the lemon juice and sea salt and freshly ground black pepper to taste.

Preheat the oven to 190°C/375°F/Gas 5. Wash and trim the fennel, reserving some of the leafy green pieces. Cut the white part into chunky pieces and cook in a little boiling salted water until just tender; drain well. Use the remaining butter to generously grease a shallow ovenproof casserole dish. Put the cooked fennel in the base of the dish and pour the lentil mixture evenly over the top. Chop up about a tablespoonful of the reserved fennel leaves and scatter them over the lentil mixture, then sprinkle with dried crumbs and grated cheese. Bake in the preheated oven for 30–40 minutes, until crunchy and golden on top and hot and bubbling underneath. For maximum utilization of protein, serve after a protein-rich first course, such as stuffed eggs, or follow this dish with a milk-based dessert.

1 onion, peeled and chopped
40g/1½oz/3tbsp butter
175g/6oz/scant 1 cup split red lentils
400ml/14fl oz/1¾ cups water or vegetable stock
1 bayleaf
juice of ½ lemon
sea salt
freshly ground black pepper
450g/1lb fennel

For the topping
a few dried crumbs
a little grated cheese

bean and vegetable pie

As it's quite time-consuming to cook the carrots, leeks and mashed potatoes specially for this dish, I try to organize things so that they get cooked as part of a previous day's meal and kept in the refrigerator until required. But in writing this recipe, I'm assuming we're starting from scratch.

serves 4

175g/6oz/scant 1 cup haricot (navy) beans
50g/2oz/¼ cup butter or margarine
1 large onion, peeled and chopped
1 large clove garlic, crushed
400ml/14fl oz/1¾ cups water or vegetable stock
2tbsp tomato paste
½tsp dried basil
sea salt
freshly ground black pepper
a little sugar
750g/1½lb potatoes, peeled
450g/1lb carrots, scraped and diced
450g/1lb leeks, cleaned and sliced
a little milk
125g/4oz/1 cup grated cheese

Soak, drain and rinse the beans as usual. Melt two-thirds of the butter in a medium-sized saucepan and fry the onion for about 10 minutes, then add the drained beans, garlic and water or stock. Bring up to the boil, then let it simmer gently for about 1 hour, until the beans are soft and the liquid reduced to a thick sauce. Stir in the tomato paste and season with basil, sea salt, freshly ground black pepper and a little sugar if necessary.

Meanwhile, cook the potatoes, carrots and leeks – the carrots and leeks can be cooked in the same saucepan; drain. Preheat the oven to 190°C /375°F/Gas 5. Mash the potatoes, using the remaining butter or margarine, a drop of milk, and sea salt and freshly ground black pepper to taste.

Grease a shallow ovenproof casserole dish and put the leeks and carrots in it. Pour the bean mixture on top, sprinkle with most of the grated cheese, then spread the mashed potato on top. Fork over the top of the potato and sprinkle with the remaining grated cheese. Bake for 30–40 minutes, until piping hot and crispy and golden on top. It's nice served with a green vegetable like spinach or broccoli.

lentil and egg bake

Another example of the excellent marriage of pulses (legumes) with hardboiled egg.
In this recipe, complementary protein is also present in the form of the wholewheat
breadcrumbs, so it's very nutritious.

serves 4–6

Set the oven to 180°C/350°F/Gas 4. Heat the oil in a
large saucepan and add the garlic, breadcrumbs and
thyme. Fry them all in the oil, stirring continuously,
until the breadcrumbs are crisp and lightly browned.
Remove from the heat and take out about a third of the
breadcrumbs. Then mix the drained cooked lentils with
the rest of the breadcrumbs in the saucepan. Season well
with freshly ground black pepper and sea salt.

Grease a shallow ovenproof dish and cover the base
with half the lentil and breadcrumb mixture. Shell and
slice the eggs and place them in a layer on top of the
lentils and breadcrumbs, then spread the remaining lentil
and breadcrumb mixture on top to cover them. Scatter
with the reserved fried breadcrumbs. Bake in the oven for
about 30 minutes, to heat everything through. A juicy
tomato salad is lovely with this.

150ml/5fl oz/⅔ cup
vegetable oil
2 large cloves garlic,
crushed
350g/12oz/6 cups fresh
wholewheat breadcrumbs
1½tsp dried thyme
225g/8oz/heaping 1 cup
green lentils, soaked,
cooked and well drained
freshly ground black pepper
sea salt
6 hardboiled eggs

lentil and mushroom slice

serves 4

175g/6oz/scant 1 cup split red lentils
350m/12fl oz/1½ cups vegetable stock or water
1 large onion
175g/6oz/2¼ cups mushrooms
25g/1oz/2tbsp butter
2tbsp chopped fresh parsley
125g/4oz/1 cup grated cheese
1 egg
sea salt
freshly ground black pepper

Put the lentils into a saucepan with the stock or water and simmer them gently until the lentils are soft and golden and all the liquid has been absorbed. Set the oven to 190°C/375°F/Gas 5.

Peel and chop the onion; wipe and slice the mushrooms. Melt the butter in a medium-sized saucepan and fry the onion and mushrooms for about 10 minutes. Add the onion and mushrooms to the lentils, together with the parsley, grated cheese and egg. Mix well and season to taste with sea salt and freshly ground black pepper. Spread the mixture into a well-greased Swiss roll tin (jelly roll pan) or similarly shaped casserole dish and bake for about 35 minutes, until set and golden brown. Serve cut in slices, with a good spicy tomato sauce, buttery potatoes and cooked vegetables.

lentil and spinach casserole

The marriage of lentils and spinach is a particularly pleasing one, and this is a nice easy casserole to make. It's good with buttery noodles or new potatoes.

serves 4

Cook the lentils in the water until they're soft and pale in colour. Meanwhile, wash the spinach carefully, then cook it in a dry saucepan for 7–10 minutes, until it's tender. Drain off the excess liquid and chop the spinach, then season it with sea salt and freshly ground black pepper. Preheat the oven to 190°C/375°F/Gas 5.

Use the butter to grease a shallow ovenproof dish generously, then put the spinach in the base and arrange the tomatoes on top. Sprinkle with sea salt and freshly ground black pepper. Season the lentils, then pour them over the tomatoes and spread them to the edges of the dish; top with a layer of grated cheese. Bake in the oven for about 40 minutes.

225g/8oz/heaping 1 cup
split red lentils
600ml/1 pint/2½ cups water
1kg/2lb spinach
sea salt
freshly ground black pepper
15g/½oz/1tbsp butter
225g/8oz tomatoes, peeled
and sliced
75–125g/3–4oz/¾–1 cup
grated cheese

musakka'a

This colourful chick pea (garbanzo bean) and aubergine (eggplant) casserole from the Middle East is lovely with fluffy brown rice or baked potatoes and a quickly cooked green vegetable. If there's any over, it's good chilled, with crusty bread and some green salad.

serves 4

150g/5oz/⅔ cup chick peas (garbanzo beans)
1kg/2lb aubergines (eggplants)
2 large onions
150ml/5fl oz/⅔ cup olive oil or vegetable oil – or a mixture
400g/14oz can tomatoes
sea salt
freshly ground black pepper

Soak, drain and rinse the chick peas (garbanzo beans) as usual. Cover with fresh cold water, cook gently until they're tender, then drain them. Wash the aubergines (eggplants) and cut them into chunky pieces.

Set the oven to 200°C/400°F/Gas 6. Peel and slice the onions and fry them in the oil in a large saucepan, then remove them with a slotted spoon and fry the aubergine (eggplant) chunks in the oil until they're crisp and lightly browned. Put the chunks into a casserole dish, together with the oil in which they were cooked, the onions, chick peas (garbanzo beans), tomatoes and a good seasoning of sea salt and freshly ground black pepper. Cover the casserole and bake it in the oven for 40–60 minutes.

red bean moussaka

This recipe was given to me by a friend, and I think it's very tasty, though I wouldn't try serving it to a Greek.

serves 4–6

Soak, cook and drain the beans as usual. Slice the aubergine (eggplant) into thin rounds. Set the oven to 180°C/350°F/Gas 4.

Fry the onion and garlic in the oil in a good-sized saucepan for about 5 minutes, but don't brown them, then add the tomatoes, tomato paste, a good grinding of pepper, the cinnamon and wine. Let the mixture cook gently for another 5 minutes or so, before mixing in the beans, mashing them slightly as you do so. Add sea salt and more freshly ground black pepper to taste if necessary.

Beat the egg into the white sauce; grease a shallow casserole dish. Put half the aubergine (eggplant) slices into the base of the dish, cover them with half the bean mixture and then half the white sauce. Repeat the layers, ending with the sauce, then sprinkle the top with the grated cheese. Bake the moussaka in the oven for about 1 hour. Serve with a green vegetable or a green salad.

225g/8oz/1⅓ cups red kidney beans
1 large aubergine (eggplant)
1 large onion, peeled and chopped
1 clove garlic, crushed
2tbsp cooking oil
3 tomatoes, peeled and chopped – or use canned
2tbsp tomato paste
freshly ground black pepper
½tsp ground cinnamon
3–4tbsp red wine
sea salt

To finish
1 egg
400ml/14fl oz/1¾ cups well-flavoured white sauce – see page 159
75g/3oz/¾ cup grated cheese

shepherds' beany pie

It's not essential to use a food processor, blender or food mill, but personally I think black eyed beans (peas) are much nicer in this type of dish if they've been puréed.

serves 4

350g/12oz/2 cups black eyed beans (peas)
2tbsp vegetable oil
1 large onion, peeled and chopped
1 clove garlic, crushed
50g/2oz/¾ cup mushrooms, wiped and chopped
225g/8oz/1 cup canned tomatoes
2tbsp tomato paste
2tbsp chopped fresh parsley
1tsp dried mixed herbs
sea salt
freshly ground black pepper

For the topping
750g/1½lb/4 cups creamy mashed potato
50g/2oz/½ cup grated cheese

Soak, drain and rinse the black eyed beans (peas) as usual. Put them into a saucepan, cover with water and cook until tender. Drain and whizz in the food processor or blender, or pass them through a food mill.

Heat the oil in a medium-sized saucepan and fry the onion and garlic for about 5 minutes, then put in the mushrooms and go on cooking for another 4–5 minutes. Add the tomatoes, tomato paste, the puréed beans (peas), parsley and mixed herbs and cook over a gentle heat for 10 minutes. Then season with sea salt and freshly ground black pepper.

Set the oven to 200°C/400°F/Gas 6. Grease a shallow ovenproof dish and put the bean mixture in the base. Spread the mashed potato evenly over the top, rough up the surface with a fork and sprinkle with grated cheese. Bake in the oven for 35–40 minutes, until golden brown and crispy.

shepherds' lentil pie

serves 4

Soak, drain and rinse the lentils as usual. Put them into a saucepan, cover with cold water and simmer gently until tender. Drain off any excess liquid.

Set the oven to 200°C/400°F/Gas 6. Fry all the vegetables in the butter in a large saucepan for 15 minutes, until they're tender, then add the lentils, herbs and tomato paste, and sea salt and freshly ground black pepper to taste. Stir well to mix.

Grease a shallow ovenproof dish and spoon in the lentil mixture; spread with the mashed potato and rough up the top with a fork. Dot with butter and bake in the oven for 30–40 minutes, until piping hot and golden brown.

225g/8oz/heaping 1 cup green lentils
1 large onion, peeled and chopped
1 clove garlic, crushed
1 celery stalk, chopped
1 large carrot, scraped and diced
125g/4oz/1½ cups mushrooms, wiped and chopped
50g/2oz/¼ cup butter
½tsp dried thyme
½tsp dried marjoram
2tbsp tomato paste
sea salt
freshly ground black pepper
750g/1½lb/4 cups creamy mashed potato

To finish
a little butter

burgers, rissoles and savoury loaves

The starchy texture of most cooked pulses (legumes) makes them ideal for forming into burgers, rissoles and loaves. A lentil rissole can be very delicious: crisp on the outside, tender and moist within, lovely with a well-flavoured sauce. Lentil or bean loaves and rolls work well too, and, as they're done in the oven, it means you can cook some crispy golden roast potatoes at the same time, to have with them – together with vegetables and a tasty gravy. Alternatively, rissoles and rolls can be served Middle Eastern fashion, with a dollop of chilled plain yogurt or, in the case of the little chick pea (garbanzo bean) balls called felafel, in pitta bread.

When cooking pulses (legumes) for burgers, rissoles, loaves and rolls, it's important not to make them too wet and mushy. Split peas and split red lentils should be cooked in just enough liquid to be absorbed during the cooking time; this means 60ml/2fl oz/¼ cup water to every 25g/1oz for unsoaked pulses (legumes) and half that quantity of water for soaked ones. The other pulses (legumes) can be drained after cooking, so the amount of water is not so crucial, but do drain them well. If necessary, dry them a little afterwards by stirring them in a saucepan over a moderate heat.

If you want a smooth-textured burger or roll, the pulses (legumes) can be puréed, though I hardly ever do this except for the felafel mixture which, being made from the firm-cooking chick peas (garbanzo beans), doesn't hold together unless it's been puréed. Apart from this, unless you're using a very tough-skinned bean, just mashing the pulses (legumes) with a fork is enough because a bit of texture seems to improve the finished dish.

If there's time, I often put the mixture into the refrigerator for half an hour or so to chill before shaping it; this firms it up and makes the job easier. For coating the rissoles, an egg and water mixture – one egg beaten with a tablespoonful of cold water – is ideal and less sticky than using all egg, and then the rissoles can be dipped in wholewheat flour or crisp dry crumbs, both of which give a good finish. Or, for a really crisp coating, dip the rissoles first into wholewheat flour, then into egg and finally into dry wholewheat breadcrumbs.

beany scotch eggs

If you use a lentil loaf mixture to encase the hardboiled eggs, you've got that very successful partnership of lentils and hardboiled eggs in a particularly attractive form.

serves 4

Make the loaf mixture and let it cool; shell the hardboiled eggs, leaving them whole.

To cover the eggs, dip them first in wholewheat flour, then in the beaten egg, then press some of the lentil mixture round them so that they are each completely covered. Next dip the covered eggs into the beaten egg again and roll them in dried crumbs. Heat the deep fat to 160°C/325°F and fry the eggs until they're crisp and golden brown all over, about 10 minutes; drain them on paper towels. Serve the eggs cut in half, with salad and perhaps some pickles.

lentil and walnut mixture –
see page 76
4 hardboiled eggs

To finish
wholewheat flour
2 eggs, beaten with 2tbsp
cold water
dried crumbs
fat for deep frying

chick pea and potato croquettes

These creamy croquettes are good served with a tomato sauce and a green vegetable.

serves 4

175g/6oz/scant 1 cup chick peas (garbanzo beans), soaked, cooked and drained
450g/1lb potatoes, cooked, drained and mashed – not too wet
1 clove garlic, crushed
½tsp paprika
2tbsp chopped fresh parsley
sea salt
freshly ground black pepper

To finish
wholewheat flour
1 egg, beaten with 1tbsp water
dry crumbs
oil for shallow frying

Mash the chick peas (garbanzo beans) roughly with a fork, then mix them with the mashed potato, crushed garlic, paprika and parsley. Season with sea salt and freshly ground black pepper.

Form the mixture into small croquettes and roll them in wholewheat flour. Dip the croquettes first into beaten egg and then into dry crumbs. Fry them in hot shallow oil; drain well on paper towels.

felafel

In the Middle East, chick peas (garbanzo beans) are used for these spicy little fritters, and very good they are too. However, I have found that split peas also make good felafel, and they are of course cheaper. These will cook to a 'mush' so that they can be mashed rather than puréed in a food processor or blender or passed through a food mill, which saves time. But only use as much water as will be absorbed during the cooking, or they will be too moist.

serves 4

Soak, drain and rinse the chick peas (garbanzo beans) as usual, cover with fresh cold water and simmer gently until very tender, 1–2 hours. Drain the chick peas (garbanzo beans) and purée them in the food processor or blender, or pass them through a fairly fine blade on a food mill.

Peel and finely grate the onion and add it to the purée, together with the spices and garlic, and sea salt and freshly ground black pepper to taste. If the mixture is rather soft, put it into the fridge for half an hour or so to firm up.

Form tablespoonfuls of the mixture into small flat cakes. Coat them well in wholewheat flour and then shallow fry them in hot oil until they're brown on both sides.

Felafel can be served Middle Eastern style with pitta bread, or English style with seasonal vegetables and a garnish of lemon and parsley. I also recommend them with the chilled yogurt and garlic sauce on page 72.

225g/8oz/heaping 1 cup
chick peas (garbanzo beans)
1 onion
1tsp ground coriander
1tsp ground cumin
good pinch of chilli powder
1 clove garlic, crushed
sea salt
freshly ground black pepper

To finish
wholewheat flour
oil for shallow frying

green pea fritters

These are really a cross between a fritter and a rissole. I usually pass the cooked peas through a food mill to remove their outer skins, but this is not essential.

serves 4

225g/8oz/heaping 1 cup dried whole green peas
2tbsp melted butter
2 eggs
125g/4oz/¾ cup + 2tbsp self-raising wholewheat flour
150ml/5fl oz/⅔ cup milk
sea salt
freshly ground black pepper

To finish
oil for shallow frying

Cover the peas with boiling water and leave them to soak for several hours. Drain and rinse them, then put them into a saucepan with more water and simmer until they're soft – about 45 minutes. Drain them if necessary, then pass them through a food mill. Add the butter, eggs, wholewheat flour and milk to the pea purée and season the mixture with sea salt and freshly ground black pepper.

Heat a little oil in a frying pan and fry spoonfuls of the mixture until crisp and brown, turning them so that both sides are cooked. Drain them well on paper towels.

These fritters are a good source of protein and I like to serve them with a tasty brown onion gravy and vegetables. Mint sauce also goes well with them.

lentil and cheese croquettes

I find that these crisp, tasty little croquettes appeal even to those who think they don't like lentils, especially if they're served with tomato sauce – see page 160. It's important to cook the lentils until they have absorbed all the water and are 'dry', or the mixture will be too moist. The flavouring can be varied according to taste: herbs such as sage are pleasant and so is a little cinnamon or curry powder.

serves 4

Wash the lentils and put them into a saucepan with the water. Simmer them for about 30 minutes, until they're tender and have absorbed all the water. Fry the onion in the oil until it's soft but not brown, then mix it in with the cooked lentils, together with the grated cheese, chilli powder, mustard and paprika, and sea salt and freshly ground black pepper to taste.

Divide the mixture into eight or twelve pieces, roll each in wholewheat flour and form it into a croquette, then dip it first into the egg and then into the wholewheat breadcrumbs.

Fry the croquettes in hot shallow oil and drain them well on paper towels. Serve them with tomato sauce – see page 160. Buttery spaghetti, noodles or potatoes also go well with this.

350g/12oz/1¾ cups split red lentils
750ml/1¼ pints/3 cups water
1 large onion, peeled and finely chopped
2tbsp oil
175g/6oz/1½ cups grated cheese
½tsp chilli powder
½tsp dry mustard
½tsp paprika
sea salt
freshly ground black pepper

To finish
wholewheat flour
1 egg, beaten with 1tbsp cold water
dry wholewheat crumbs
oil for shallow frying

lentil and egg burgers

Green lentils and hardboiled eggs are one of those great combinations, like basil and tomatoes and sage and onion. I particularly like them together in these crisp burgers.

serves 4

225g/8oz/heaping 1 cup green lentils
300ml/10fl oz/1¼ cups water
1 large onion
50g/2oz/¼ cup butter
4 hardboiled eggs
2tbsp finely chopped fresh parsley
½tsp ground mace or a little grated nutmeg
sea salt
freshly ground black pepper

To finish
wholewheat flour
oil for shallow frying

Soak, drain and rinse the lentils as usual, then cover them with the water and cook them gently until they're soft and have absorbed the water. Meanwhile, peel and finely chop the onion and fry it in the butter for about 10 minutes until it's tender and golden brown. Shell and chop the hardboiled eggs and mix them in with the cooked lentils, together with the onion, parsley, mace or nutmeg and sea salt and freshly ground black pepper to taste. Let the mixture cool, then shape it into eight round burgers and roll them in wholewheat flour. Fry the burgers in hot shallow oil until they're crisp on both sides; drain them on paper towels.

These are lovely served with some plain or garlic mayonnaise, or with yogurt and a crunchy cabbage, carrot, sweet green pepper and pineapple salad. Or serve them with creamy mashed potatoes, cooked vegetables and a good gravy.

lentil and onion rissoles with mint sauce

The sharpness of the sauce goes well with the lentils. Serve these rissoles with cooked vegetables and mashed potatoes for a complete meal.

serves 4

Put the lentils into a good-sized saucepan with the water and cook them gently for about 30 minutes, until they're soft and pale. Fry the onion in the butter for 10 minutes, letting it brown lightly. Add the fried onion and the egg to the cooked lentils, mashing the lentils a bit as you do so. Flavour with sea salt, freshly ground black pepper and lemon juice. Form the mixture – which should be fairly stiff – into little rounds and roll them in wholewheat flour. Fry them on both sides in hot shallow oil and drain them on paper towels. Serve them with a sauce made by mixing together the mint, boiling water, sugar and vinegar. I usually do this by whizzing them all in the food processor or blender for a minute or two, and this means there's no need to chop the mint: you can put in the whole sprigs with just any tough stems removed.

350g/12oz/1¾ cups split red lentils
750ml/1¼ pints/ 3 cups water
1 large onion, peeled and chopped
25g/1oz/2tbsp butter
1 egg
sea salt
freshly ground black pepper
2tbsp lemon juice

To finish
wholewheat flour for coating
oil for shallow frying

For the sauce
2 rounded tbsp chopped fresh mint
2tbsp boiling water
2tbsp sugar
2tbsp cider vinegar or white wine vinegar

lentil rissoles with yogurt sauce

I think these spicy rissoles are best with a chilled yogurt sauce, but you could serve them with a hot tomato or curry sauce. They're good with fluffy brown rice and a green salad.

serves 4

225g/8oz/heaping 1 cup split red lentils
400ml/14fl oz/1¾ cups water
1 onion
2tbsp oil
½tsp ground cumin
½tsp ground coriander
½tsp turmeric
1 egg
2tbsp lemon juice
sea salt
freshly ground black pepper

To finish
wholewheat flour
oil for shallow frying

For the sauce
300ml/10fl oz/1¼ cups plain yogurt
2tbsp chopped fresh parsley
1 clove garlic, crushed

Put the lentils and water into a medium-sized saucepan and cook them for about 30 minutes, until the lentils are pale and soft and all the water has been absorbed.

Peel and finely chop the onion, fry in the oil for about 10 minutes, until it's soft, then put in the spices and fry for a further 2–3 minutes. Add the onion and spices to the lentils, together with the egg, lemon juice and seasoning to taste. Mix it all together well, then form it into small rissoles and coat each one with wholewheat flour.

Heat a little oil in a frying pan and fry the rissoles until they're crisp, then drain them on paper towels and keep them warm.

Make the sauce by mixing together the yogurt, parsley and garlic. Season with sea salt and freshly ground black pepper and serve with the rissoles.

spicy lentil burgers

These burgers are good with some buttery noodles or brown rice and a well-flavoured curry or tomato sauce. They're also nice cold, with plain yogurt, mango chutney and salad.

serves 3–4

Soak, drain and rinse the lentils as usual, then put them into a medium-sized saucepan with the water. Simmer them gently until they're tender and have absorbed all the liquid, 30–45 minutes.

Meanwhile, heat the oil in a medium-sized saucepan and fry the onion for 5 minutes or so, then add the garlic and green pepper and cook for a further 5 minutes. Stir in the spices and let them cook for another minute or two. Add the fried vegetables and spices to the cooked lentils, season with sea salt and freshly ground black pepper and then leave the mixture to get cold. Form into burgers and dip them first into the beaten egg and then into dried crumbs. Fry the burgers in hot shallow oil until crisp on both sides, then drain them on paper towels.

225g/8oz/heaping 1 cup green lentils
300ml/10fl oz/1¼ cups water
2tbsp oil
1 large onion, peeled and chopped
1 large clove garlic, crushed
1 small sweet green pepper, deseeded and chopped
1tsp turmeric
1tsp ground coriander
1tsp ground cumin
¼–½tsp chilli powder
sea salt
freshly ground black pepper

To finish
1 egg, beaten with 1tbsp water
dried crumbs
shallow oil for frying

soya bean and egg croquettes

There's no problem about protein here: these tasty little croquettes are as nutritious as any beef steak.

serves 3–4

125g/4oz/heaping ½ cup soya beans (soybeans), soaked, well rinsed, cooked until very tender and drained

1 onion, peeled and finely chopped

1 clove garlic, crushed

25g/1oz/2tbsp butter

4 hardboiled eggs

50g/2oz/1 cup wholewheat breadcrumbs

2tbsp tomato paste

2tbsp chopped fresh parsley

½tsp ground mace

1 egg

sea salt

freshly ground black pepper

To finish

wholewheat flour

beaten egg

dried crumbs

oil for shallow frying

Mash the beans with a fork, just to break them up. Fry the onion and garlic in the butter for 10 minutes, then remove from the heat and stir in the beans. Shell the hardboiled eggs, then chop them fairly finely and add them to the beans, together with the wholewheat breadcrumbs, tomato paste, chopped parsley, mace and egg. Mix well, then taste and season. Form the mixture into little croquettes, roll them in wholewheat flour, then dip them into beaten egg and roll them in dried crumbs. Fry the croquettes in hot shallow oil and drain them well on paper towels. They're nice with a spicy tomato sauce.

variation

Soya bean (soybean) and walnut croquettes are good, too. Omit the egg and use instead 125g/4oz/1 cup walnuts, pulverized in the food processor or blender, and ½tsp dried thyme. You may need to add a little more liquid to the mixture – or don't use all the breadcrumbs.

split pea fritters with apple rings

Fruit goes surprisingly well with pulses (legumes). Here there is also a pleasant contrast of texture: soft apple rings against crisp fritters.

serves 4

Soak, drain and rinse the split peas as usual. Put them into a saucepan with the water and cook them until they're tender. Drain if necessary and dry by stirring over a moderate heat for a minute or two.

Fry the onion in the butter in a large saucepan for 10 minutes, then add the sage, split peas, ground cloves and egg. Mix well, mashing the split peas a bit with the spoon, then season with sea salt and freshly ground black pepper, and add a little lemon juice if you think the mixture needs it.

Shape the split pea mixture into 12 small rounds on a floured board, then dip each in egg and dry crumbs; coat well. Fry the fritters in hot shallow oil until they're crisp on both sides; drain them on paper towels and keep warm.

To make the apple rings, peel the apples and remove the cores using an apple corer, keeping the apples whole. Then slice the apples into thin rings. Heat the butter and 2 tbsp oil in a clean frying pan and fry the apple rings for a minute or two on each side to cook them through and brown them lightly. Serve the fritters with the apple rings.

350g/12oz/1½ cups yellow
split peas
400ml/14fl oz/1¾ cups water
1 large onion, peeled and
chopped
25g/1oz/2tbsp butter
½tsp dried **sage**
pinch of ground cloves
1 egg
sea salt
freshly ground black pepper
a little lemon juice

To finish
wholewheat flour
1 egg, beaten with 1tbsp
water
dried crumbs
oil for shallow frying
2 medium-sized cooking
(tart) apples
25g/1oz/2tbsp butter

lentil and walnut loaf

People usually find it difficult to guess what this loaf is made from: the result is tasty and 'chewy' and of course it's packed with protein. It's nice served hot with roast potatoes, gravy and vegetables, or cold with some mayonnaise or chutney.

serves 4–6

175g/6oz/scant 1 cup green lentils
1 onion, peeled and chopped up small
1 large clove garlic, crushed
2tbsp oil
1tsp dried thyme
125g/4oz/1 cup walnuts, ground or pulverized in the food processor or blender
125g/4oz/2 cups wholewheat breadcrumbs
2tbsp tomato paste
2tbsp chopped fresh parsley
1 egg
sea salt
freshly ground black pepper

To serve
1 tomato, sliced
a sprig of parsley

Soak the lentils for a few hours, then rinse them and put them into a saucepan with enough cold water to cover. Simmer gently for about 40 minutes, until they're tender, then drain off any liquid.

Prepare a 450g/1lb loaf pan (measuring about 18 x 10 x 7.5cm/6 x 4 x 3 inches). Put a long strip of foil across the bottom and up the two narrow sides; grease the inside of the pan and the foil generously with butter. Set the oven to 190°C/375°F/ Gas 5.

Fry the onion and garlic in the oil in a good-sized saucepan for 10 minutes until tender and lightly browned. Stir in the thyme and fry for a few seconds, then remove the saucepan from the heat and add the lentils, walnuts, wholewheat breadcrumbs, tomato paste, parsley and egg. Mix well, then season with sea salt and freshly ground black pepper. Spoon the mixture into the prepared pan and smooth the top. Cover with a piece of greased foil and bake in the oven for 1 hour. Leave the loaf to stand in its pan for a minute or two after removing it from the oven, then slip a knife round the edges of the loaf to loosen it and turn it out; strip off the foil. Garnish the top of the loaf with slices of tomato and a sprig of parsley.

soya loaf

This is my adaptation of an American recipe that was given to me. It makes a tasty loaf, and of course it's very rich in protein.

serves 4–5

Soak, drain, rinse and cook the beans as usual – they will take about 4 hours to get really soft. Then drain and mash them. Preheat the oven to 190°C/375°F/Gas 5.

Fry the onion, garlic and celery in the butter in a good-sized saucepan for about 15 minutes, until they're all tender, then add the tomatoes and tomato paste and cook gently for a further 5 minutes. Stir in the beans, wholewheat breadcrumbs, parsley, thyme and egg and season the mixture carefully with sea salt and freshly ground black pepper.

Prepare a 450g/1lb loaf pan (measuring about 18 x 10 x 7.5cm/6 x 4 x 3 inches). Grease it very generously with butter, then coat with dried crumbs, which should stick to the butter. This will help the loaf to come out of the pan easily and make the outside nice and crisp. Spoon the loaf mix into the pan and smooth down the top. Cover with a piece of buttered foil and bake in the oven for 1 hour. Let the loaf stand for a minute or so, then slip a knife round the edges and turn it out on to a warm dish. Serve with roast potatoes, gravy and vegetables. Apple sauce goes well with it too.

175g/6oz/scant 1 cup soya beans (soybeans)
1 large onion, peeled and chopped
2 cloves garlic, crushed
4 celery stalks, washed and chopped
50g/2oz/¼ cup butter
2 tomatoes, peeled and chopped
2tbsp tomato paste
125g/4oz/2 cups whole-wheat breadcrumbs
4tbsp chopped fresh parsley
1tsp dried thyme
1 egg
sea salt
freshly ground black pepper

To finish
a little butter
dried crumbs

crêpes and pasta

You might think that the combination of pulses (legumes) and crêpes or pasta would be definitely erring on the side of stodge, but, if the dish is well cooked, this is not the case. In fact this combination is, in my opinion, one of the best.

Light, feathery crêpes wrapped round a moist, tasty bean mixture and topped with a cheese sauce, or a succulent lasagne layered with a rich lentil paste makes very tasty eating indeed. They are also extremely satisfying, bringing together as they do the two complementary proteins, pulse (legume) and wheat, not to mention the extra dairy proteins which are also included, so they provide excellent nourishment tastily and economically.

Although the list of ingredients in these recipes may look a bit long and daunting, don't let this deter you. Usually these dishes can be made in several easy-going stages, which can be fitted in with other tasks, so that with a little forward planning they are not really too irksome.

chilli red bean crêpes

It's up to you how 'hot' you make the chilli red bean filling, but start with the smaller quantity of chilli powder and taste as you go.

serves 4

Make the filling. Put the beans into a saucepan with the water and boil them vigorously for 10 minutes then lower the heat and cook them gently until they're tender, about 1 hour. Drain them, reserving the cooking liquid.

Preheat the oven to 180°C/350°F/Gas 4. Heat the oil in a medium-sized saucepan and fry the onion for 10 minutes, but don't let it get brown. Add the garlic, bayleaf, oregano, tomatoes, tomato paste and chilli powder and let it all simmer gently, uncovered, for about 15 minutes. Add half of this tomato mixture to the cooked beans, mashing them roughly. Season with sea salt, freshly ground black pepper and, if necessary, more chilli powder to taste. Spread about 2tbsp of this bean mixture on each crêpe, roll them up and place them side by side in a well-greased, shallow ovenproof dish.

Mix the rest of the tomato mixture with the reserved bean liquor – there should be just under 150ml/5fl oz/ ⅔ cup. Season to taste, then pour this over the crêpes and sprinkle the top with grated cheese. Put the dish into the oven for about 30 minutes, to heat it through and brown the top. It's lovely served with buttery spinach or broccoli.

10–12 thin crêpes – see page 161

For the filling and sauce
175g/6oz/1 cup red kidney beans, soaked for several hours in cold water, then drained and rinsed
600ml/1 pint/2½ cups water
2tbsp oil
2 onions, peeled and chopped
2 cloves garlic, crushed
1 bayleaf
½tsp dried oregano
400g/14oz can tomatoes
1tbsp tomato paste
¼–1tsp chilli powder
sea salt
freshly ground black pepper

For the topping
125g/4oz/1 cup grated cheese

crêpes with flageolets mushrooms and artichokes

Use frozen artichoke bottoms if you can get them – they are often sold in Middle Eastern stores – otherwise use 2 x 400g/14oz cans artichoke hearts, drained.

serves 6

10–12 thin crêpes – see page 161

For the filling and topping
225g/8oz/heaping 1 cup flageolet beans, soaked overnight in cold water
350g/12oz/4½ cups button mushrooms
2 cloves garlic
50g/2oz/¼ cup butter
450g/1lb frozen artichoke bottoms, thawed
175g/6oz/¾ cup cream cheese
2tbsp chopped fresh parsley
sea salt
freshly ground black pepper
400ml/14fl oz/1¾ cups cheese sauce – see page 159
50g/2oz/½ cup grated cheese
a few dried crumbs

Make the filling. Drain and rinse the flageolets, then put them into a saucepan with a good covering of cold water. Simmer them gently for about 1 hour, until they're tender, then drain them. Preheat the oven to 180°C/350°F/Gas 4.

Wipe and slice the mushrooms and peel and crush the garlic, then fry them in the butter for 4–5 minutes, until the mushrooms are tender. Roughly chop the artichoke bottoms and add them to the mushrooms, together with the cooked flageolets, cream cheese, parsley and seasoning; mix well.

Spread the crêpes with the filling, then roll them up and place them side by side in a buttered shallow casserole dish. Pour the sauce over the crêpes and sprinkle the grated cheese and crumbs on top. Bake the crêpes in the oven for 35–40 minutes until lightly browned on top.

crêpes with lentil and mushroom filling

It's alright to cook the lentils with the tomatoes because they're quick-cooking. There's also stock to take off some of the acidity which can prevent pulses (legumes) from softening.

serves 4–6

Make the filling. Peel and chop the onion; crush the garlic. Fry them together in the butter and oil in a medium-sized saucepan for 5 minutes, then stir in the lentils, water or stock, tomatoes, cumin and wine. Let the mixture simmer gently, uncovered, for 30 minutes. Add the mushrooms and cook for a further 5–6 minutes, then season with sea salt and freshly ground black pepper. Preheat the oven to 180°C/350°F/Gas 4.

Spread a little of the lentil mixture on each crêpe; roll the crêpes up neatly and arrange them side by side in a well-greased, shallow ovenproof dish. Pour the sauce over the crêpe rolls, sprinkle with grated cheese and bake in the oven for 30–40 minutes.

10–12 thin crêpes – see page 161

For the filling and topping
1 large onion
2 cloves garlic
25g/1oz/2tbsp butter
2tbsp oil
175g/6 oz/scant 1 cup split red lentils
300ml/10fl oz/1¼ cups water or vegetable stock
400g/14oz can tomatoes
½tsp ground cumin
2tbsp red wine
225g/8oz/3 cups button mushrooms, wiped and sliced
sea salt
freshly ground black pepper
400ml/14fl oz/1¾ cups white sauce – see page 159
50g/2oz/½ cup grated cheese

indian rice crêpes with split pea filling

These Indian crêpes are different from the others in this section because the batter is made from a mixture of rice, milk and split peas and contains no eggs. This gives a delicious, rather nutty flavour, and a slightly different texture. I find it best to make the crêpes fairly small – certainly using no more than two tablespoonfuls of batter per crêpe – as they are then more manageable.

A food processor or blender is essential for this recipe – unless you want to spend hours grinding up the rice and peas – and you need to start preparations the day before you want to make it. I've tried the crêpes without the fermentation period and they don't work as well, so it's best to be patient.

serves 4

225g/8oz/heaping 1 cup long grain brown rice
225g/8oz/1 cup yellow split peas
1tsp sea salt
300ml/10fl oz/1¼ cups water
300ml/10fl oz/1¼ cups milk and water mixed
oil for frying
1 onion, peeled and chopped
1 clove garlic, crushed
1tsp ground cumin
1tsp turmeric
2tsp lemon juice
freshly ground black pepper

Put the brown rice and split peas into separate bowls, cover them well with cold water and leave to soak overnight. Next day, rinse them and remove one-third of the split peas; cover these with cold water and cook them until they're tender, then set them aside for the crêpe filling. Put the remaining split peas and all the rice into the food processor or blender, together with the water and 1tsp sea salt, and whizz them together to a smooth, creamy paste. Turn the paste into a bowl and leave in a warm place for 12 hours, or overnight, to ferment. Next day, add the milk and water to the paste and whip it until smooth and creamy.

To make the crêpes, heat a little oil in a frying pan and pour in 1–2tbsp of the batter. I find these crêpes take a little longer to cook than the ordinary type, and if you try to turn them over too soon they will collapse. So let the

crêpe cook thoroughly underneath and test it by lifting
the edge with a palette knife (metal spatula). If it feels
firm and looks brown, carefully turn it over and cook the
other side. Repeat with the remaining batter

I usually serve these crispy crêpes flat, with the filling
simply spooned on top, but they can be rolled round the
filling and placed side by side in a shallow dish if you prefer.
They are not difficult to do once you get used to the texture.

To make the filling, fry the onion and garlic with the
spices in 2tbsp oil for about 10 minutes, without
browning, then stir in the reserved cooked split peas and
heat through. Add lemon juice to taste and season with
sea salt and freshly ground black pepper.

The mixture of rice and split peas is of course excellent
from the nutritional point of view because it brings
together two complementary proteins.

crêpes with spinach and lentil filling

serves 4–6

10–12 thin crêpes
– see page 161

For the lentil filling
125g/4oz/heaping ½ cup
green lentils, soaked
overnight in cold water
2tbsp oil
25g/1oz/2tbsp butter
1 onion, peeled and chopped
1 clove garlic, crushed
175g/6oz/2¼ cups
mushrooms, wiped and sliced
1tbsp tomato paste
sea salt
freshly ground black pepper

For the spinach filling
450g/1lb spinach
15g/½oz/1tbsp butter
grated nutmeg

To finish
400ml/14fl oz/1¾ cups
cheese sauce – see page 159
75g/3oz/¾ cup grated cheese

Make the lentil filling. Drain and rinse the lentils, put them into a saucepan with cold water to cover and simmer for about 40 minutes, until they're tender. Meanwhile, heat the oil and butter in another saucepan and fry the onion and garlic for 5 minutes, then add the mushrooms and cook for another 5 minutes. Drain the lentils and add them to the onion and mushroom mixture, together with the tomato paste and some sea salt and freshly ground black pepper.

For the spinach filling, wash the spinach thoroughly in three changes of water, then cook it as usual in a dry saucepan over rather a high heat for about 7–10 minutes, until it's tender. Drain and chop the spinach, then add the butter and a good seasoning of salt, pepper and nutmeg.

Preheat the oven to 180°C/350°F/Gas 4. Put a rounded tablespoon of lentil mixture in the middle of a crêpe and roll the crêpe round it. Repeat until you've used up all the lentil mixture and half the crêpes, then fill the remaining crêpes with spinach in the same way. Arrange the crêpes in a well-greased, shallow ovenproof dish, alternating the two types. Pour the cheese sauce evenly over them and sprinkle with grated cheese, then bake for 30–40 minutes, until piping hot and golden brown on top.

tuoni e lampo

The Italian name of this dish means 'thunder and lightning' and refers to the texture of the two main ingredients, the soft pasta and the firm chick peas (garbanzo beans). It is very tasty, but you really do need to use olive oil to give the right flavour. Traditionally it is made with different shapes of white pasta, but I generally use one of the wholewheat ones because I think they're healthier.

serves 4

Soak, drain and rinse the chick peas (garbanzo beans) as usual. Put them into a saucepan with a good covering of fresh cold water and simmer them gently until they're tender. Drain the chick peas (garbanzo beans) and keep them warm. Cook the macaroni in boiling salted water, until it's just tender, then drain it. Heat the olive oil in a large saucepan and add the garlic, chick peas (garbanzo beans) and pasta, together with sea salt and freshly ground black pepper to taste. Toss them gently together until everything is glossy with the oil. Serve immediately, with a good sprinkling of cheese and a tossed green salad.

225g/8oz/heaping 1 cup
chick peas (garbanzo beans)
225g/8oz/heaping 1¾ cups
thin macaroni
sea salt
4tbsp olive oil
1 large clove garlic, crushed
freshly ground black pepper

To serve
plenty of dry, grated cheese

spaghetti with green lentil sauce

Pulses (legumes) make lovely sauces for spaghetti, and the use of a pressure cooker can put this kind of dish into the 'quick meal' class. It's very nourishing and satisfying too.

serves 4

175g/6oz/scant 1 cup green lentils
1 onion
2 cloves garlic
2tbsp oil
125g/4oz/1½ cups mushrooms, wiped and sliced
1 small sweet green pepper, deseeded and chopped
2 tomatoes, peeled and chopped
1tbsp red wine
1tbsp tomato paste
1tsp ground coriander
pinch of chilli powder
sea salt
freshly ground black pepper
225g/8oz spaghetti
15g/½oz/1tbsp butter

To serve
grated cheese

If there's time to get organized in advance, soak the lentils in cold water for a few hours, then drain and rinse them. If you're in a hurry, just wash the lentils. Put them into a saucepan, cover with cold water and simmer gently until they're tender – about 40 minutes if they've been soaked, 1–1¼ hours if not, or around 15 minutes in a pressure cooker.

Meanwhile, peel and chop the onion and crush the garlic. Fry them together in the oil for 5 minutes, then add the mushrooms and green pepper and cook for a further 5 minutes or so. Drain the lentils and stir them into the vegetable mixture, together with the tomatoes, wine, tomato paste and seasonings. Let the mixture simmer gently while you cook the spaghetti in plenty of boiling salted water. Drain it when it's just tender, put it back into the hot saucepan and add the butter, turning the spaghetti until the butter has melted and the spaghetti looks all glossy and appetizing. Then turn the spaghetti on to a warm serving dish, pour the lentil sauce on top of it and sprinkle with grated cheese. This is lovely served with a crisp green salad.

spaghetti with lentil and tomato sauce

As split red lentils cook in under half an hour without soaking, this dish is useful for those times when you suddenly find yourself having to produce a meal quickly, particularly as the ingredients are basic storecupboard ones.

serves 4

Heat the oil in a largish saucepan and fry the onion and garlic until they're tender – about 10 minutes. Add the tomatoes, herbs, cinnamon, lentils, water and wine and bring up to the boil, then simmer the mixture with a lid on the saucepan for about 25 minutes, until the lentils are tender. Taste, and season with sea salt and freshly ground black pepper.

About 10 minutes before the lentils are done, start cooking the spaghetti. Half-fill a large saucepan with water, add some sea salt and bring to the boil. Add the spaghetti to the saucepan by holding it upright in the boiling water and gradually pushing it down into the water as it softens. Simmer the spaghetti until it's just tender, or *al dente* as the Italians say, then drain it and add the butter and a good grinding of black pepper. Pile the spaghetti on to a warm serving dish, pour the sauce on top and sprinkle with grated cheese. Serve with a nice crisp green salad.

2tbsp oil
1 large onion, peeled and chopped
1 large clove garlic, crushed
400g/14oz can tomatoes
½tsp dried basil or oregano
½tsp ground cinnamon
225g/8oz/heaping 1 cup split red lentils, washed
400ml/14fl oz/1¾ cups water
2tbsp red wine – if possible
sea salt
freshly ground black pepper
225g/8oz spaghetti
15g/½oz/1tbsp butter

To serve
a little grated cheese

pastichio

Strictly speaking, pastichio should be made with a layer of pasta, a layer of spicy beef mince mixture, a thick cream sauce and a thin cream sauce. My version consists of the pasta and spicy lentils topped with a creamy sauce.

serves 6

1 large onion
2–3 cloves garlic
1 small sweet green pepper
125g/4oz/1½ cups mushrooms
50g/2oz/¼ cup butter
400g/14oz can tomatoes
225g/8oz/heaping 1 cup split red lentils, washed
½tsp dried oregano
½tsp ground cinnamon
½ glass red wine
400ml/14fl oz/1¾ cups water or vegetable stock
sea salt
freshly ground black pepper
175g/6oz/1½ cups macaroni
2 eggs
400ml/14fl oz/1¾ cups well-flavoured white sauce – see page 159
75g/3oz/¾ cup grated cheese

Peel and chop the onion; crush the garlic. Deseed and chop the green pepper. Wipe and slice the mushrooms. Melt the butter in a large saucepan and fry the onion for 5 minutes then add the garlic, green pepper and mushrooms and cook for a further 5 minutes or so, stirring from time to time. Mix in the tomatoes, lentils, oregano, cinnamon, wine and water or stock. Bring up to the boil, give it a good stir, then simmer gently for about 45 minutes, until the lentils are soft and the liquid has boiled away to leave a lovely thick, rich mixture. Season carefully with sea salt and freshly ground black pepper and add a little more cinnamon and oregano if you think it can take it – the mixture should be quite highly seasoned.

When the lentils are nearly done, set the oven to 200°C/400°F/Gas 6, then cook the macaroni by plunging it into a saucepan of fast-boiling salted water and boiling until it's just tender. Drain the macaroni and put it into a well-buttered, shallow oblong ovenproof dish. Spoon the lentil mixture on top. Beat the eggs into the white sauce, then pour that evenly over the lentils and sprinkle with the grated cheese. Bake the pastichio in the middle of the oven for 40–50 minutes, until it's piping hot with a lovely golden brown top. Serve with a herby green salad.

lentil lasagne

This is a lovely tasty dish, packed with protein. Serve it with a salad or buttery French (fine green) beans or broccoli.

serves 6–8

Wash and pick over the lentils, then cover them with cold water and leave them to soak for several hours. Fry the onion and garlic in the butter and oil in a medium-sized saucepan for 10 minutes, then add the lentils and stir for a minute or two so that the lentils are coated with the garlic and fat. Mix in the water or stock, bring up to the boil and simmer gently, uncovered, for about 45 minutes, when the lentils should be tender and the mixture thick. Mix in the coriander and season with sea salt and freshly ground black pepper.

Set the oven to 200°C/400°F/Gas 6. Cook the lasagne in boiling salted water until it's tender, then drain it well. Beat the eggs into the white sauce.

Put half the lentil mixture into the base of a well-greased, shallow ovenproof casserole dish. Arrange half the lasagne slices on top, then pour in half the sauce mixture. Repeat the layers, ending with the sauce, and sprinkle the top with grated cheese. Bake in the middle of the oven for 40–50 minutes, until bubbling and golden.

350g/12oz/1¾ cups green lentils
1 large onion, peeled and chopped
2 cloves garlic, crushed
25g/1oz/2tbsp butter
2tbsp oil
600ml/1 pint /2½ cups water or vegetable stock
1tsp ground coriander
sea salt
freshly ground black pepper
225g/8oz lasagne

For the topping
2 eggs
600ml/1 pint /2½ cups well-flavoured white sauce – see page 159
125g/4oz/1 cup grated cheese

spaghetti and bean bake

Tasty, filling and full of protein, this really only needs a green salad to go with it.

serves 6

175g/6oz/scant 1 cup
haricot (navy) beans or
butter or lima beans
2 large onions
2 large cloves garlic
125g/4oz/1½ cups
mushrooms
4tbsp olive oil
2 x 400g/14oz cans tomatoes
3tbsp tomato paste
2tbsp red wine – if available
1tsp dried oregano or basil
1tsp ground cinnamon
2–3tbsp chopped fresh
parsley
½tsp chilli powder
sea salt
freshly ground black pepper
sugar
175g/6oz thin spaghetti

To finish
dried crumbs
a little grated cheese
a little butter

Soak, rinse and cook the beans as usual, then drain them.

Next, make a tomato sauce. Peel and chop the onions; crush the garlic. Wipe and chop the mushrooms. Fry the onions and garlic in the olive oil in a largish saucepan for 10 minutes, then stir in the mushrooms and cook for a further 4–5 minutes. Add the tomatoes, tomato paste, the red wine if you're using it, and the oregano or basil, cinnamon, parsley and chilli powder. Let the sauce simmer, without a lid on the saucepan, for 10 minutes or so, until the vegetables are all cooked and the liquid has reduced to a thickish paste. Season with sea salt, freshly ground black pepper and a little sugar to taste.

Preheat the oven to 180°C/350°F/Gas 4. Cook the spaghetti in plenty of boiling salted water until it's just tender, then drain it well.

Grease a 1.75 litre/3 pint/3¾ pint shallow ovenproof casserole and spread a layer of half the spaghetti in the base; arrange half the beans on top and pour in half the sauce. Repeat the layers, ending with a layer of sauce. Sprinkle generously with crumbs and grated cheese; dot with butter. Bake in the oven for 45–50 minutes, until golden and crisp on top.

pastry dishes

If pulses (legumes) and pastry are going to be really delicious together, they've both got to be light. Solid lentils in heavy pastry would be dreary beyond belief. But a quiche of tender beans, mushrooms and onions in a light, well-flavoured custard on a crisp pastry base, or well-cooked butter or lima beans with leeks and tomatoes topped with golden puff pastry, are another thing altogether and always seem to go down well.

I generally use frozen puff pastry, but shortcrust (pie) pastry is quick and easy to make, especially if you use a food processor. The basic recipe is on page 162.

bean and leek pie

This makes a lovely family meal. Serve it with a cooked green vegetable and potatoes, too, if you're catering for a hungry, growing family.

serves 4

125g/4oz/heaping ½ cup butter or lima beans
50g/2oz/¼ cup butter
225g/8oz/1½ cups carrots, scraped and diced small
450g/1lb leeks, cleaned and cut into 1cm/½ inch slices
125g/4oz/1½ cups mushrooms, wiped and sliced
1tbsp flour
225g/8oz/1 cup canned tomatoes
150ml/5fl oz/⅔ cup vegetable stock
sea salt
freshly ground black pepper

For the pie crust
225g/8oz puff pastry
a little beaten egg to glaze, if liked

Soak, drain and rinse the beans as usual, then cook them until they're tender and drain well.

Preheat the oven to 220°C/425°F/Gas 7. Melt the butter in a medium-sized saucepan, then put in the carrots, cover and cook very gently without browning for 10 minutes. Add the leeks and mushrooms and cook for a further 10 minutes. Sprinkle in the flour then stir so that it gets mixed with the fat. Mix in the tomatoes and stock and cook gently, stirring, for 2–3 minutes, until thickened. Add the beans to the saucepan and season with sea salt and freshly ground black pepper. Turn the mixture into a 1.2 litre/2 pint/1¼ quart pie dish; cool.

Roll out the pastry on a lightly floured board and use it to cover the top of the pie. Crimp the edges and decorate the top of the pie with little pastry cut-outs if you're feeling that way inclined. Brush the surface of the pastry with beaten egg if you want a shiny finish. Bake in the preheated oven for 20 minutes, then reduce the heat to 190°C/ 375°F/ Gas 5 and bake for a further 15 minutes.

bean and tomato pie

The wholewheat crust gives this pie an attractive rustic look, but it's also good made with puff pastry, like the bean and leek pie.

serves 4

Soak, drain and rinse the beans as usual. Cover with cold water and cook until tender, then drain.

Preheat the oven to 220°C/425°F/Gas 7. Peel and chop the onion and fry it in the butter for 10 minutes, then add the tomato paste, tomatoes and basil, and a seasoning of sea salt, freshly ground black pepper and a little sugar if you think it needs it. Simmer gently for 10 minutes. Mix in the beans, check seasoning and pour into a 1.2 litre/2 pint/1¼ quart pie dish.

Roll out the pastry and use it to cover the top of the pie. Crimp the edges and decorate the top as required. Brush the surface of the pastry with beaten egg if you want a shiny finish. Bake the pie in the preheated oven for 20 minutes, then turn the heat down to 190°C/375°F/Gas 5 and bake for a further 10–15 minutes.

175g/6oz/scant 1 cup butter or lima beans
1 large onion
50g/2oz/¼ cup butter
1tbsp tomato paste
400g/14oz can tomatoes
½tsp dried basil
sea salt
freshly ground black pepper
a little sugar

For the pie crust
1 quantity of shortcrust (pie) pastry – see page 162
beaten egg to glaze, if liked

lentil and tomato pie

serves 4–6

1 large onion
50g/2oz/¼ cup butter
175g/6oz/scant 1 cup split red lentils
1 large clove garlic, crushed
350ml/12fl oz/1½ cups vegetable stock or water
2 tomatoes, peeled and chopped
75g/3oz/¾ cup grated cheese
1tsp dried basil
1tbsp lemon juice
1 egg
sea salt
freshly ground black pepper

For the pie crust
1 quantity of shortcrust (pie) pastry – see page 162
a little beaten egg to glaze, if liked

First make the filling: peel and chop the onion and fry it in the butter in a good-sized saucepan until it's golden and beginning to soften, about 5–6 minutes. Add the split red lentils and garlic and stir for a moment or two before adding the stock or water. Bring the mixture up to the boil, half-cover with a lid and simmer for about 20 minutes, until the lentils are soft and pale golden. Remove the saucepan from the heat and add the tomatoes, cheese, basil, lemon juice and egg, and sea salt and freshly ground black pepper to taste. Leave the mixture to cool.

Roll out about two-thirds of the pastry and use to line a 20cm/8 inch quiche dish or sandwich (layer cake) pan. Roll the remainder into a circle to fit the top of the dish. Preheat the oven to 200°C/400°F/Gas 6. Spread the lentil mixture in the pastry case. Dampen the edges of the pastry with a little cold water, then put the circle of pastry on top and press down lightly, crimping the edges. Prick the top and brush with a little beaten egg if you want a shiny finish. Bake the pie in the preheated oven for about 40 minutes, until golden brown and crisp.

bean and onion quiche

This is a tasty quiche, packed with protein.

serves 4–6

Preheat the oven to 220°C/425°F/Gas 7. Roll out the pastry and use it to line a 20cm/8 inch quiche dish. Prick the base of the quiche, then bake it in the oven for about 15 minutes, until firm and crisp. Turn the oven heat down to 180°C/350°F/Gas 4.

Peel and slice the onion and fry it in the butter for about 10 minutes, until it's soft but not browned. Mix together the cheese and mustard. Beat the egg with the milk and season with sea salt and freshly ground black pepper. Put the hot cooked onion straight into the hot quiche case and arrange the beans on top. Sprinkle with the cheese and mustard mixture, then pour in the egg and milk and scatter with the chopped parsley. Bake for 40–50 minutes, until set and golden brown. I think it's nicest served hot or warm, but you can also serve it cold. You can freeze it, too, but the pastry is never as crisp afterwards, I find.

1 quantity of shortcrust
(pie) pastry – see page 162

For the filling
1 large onion
25g/1oz/2tbsp butter
125g/4oz/1 cup grated
cheese
1tsp dry mustard
1 egg
150ml/5fl oz/⅔ cup milk
sea salt
freshly ground black pepper
125g/4oz/heaping ½ cup
butter or lima beans,
soaked, cooked and then
drained
1tbsp chopped fresh parsley

chick pea and mushroom quiche

I think this quiche is best served hot, with a crisp salad or cooked green vegetable.

serves 6

1 quantity of shortcrust
(pie) pastry – see page 162

For the filling
25g/1oz/2tbsp butter
1 onion, peeled and sliced
1 large clove garlic, crushed
125g/4oz/1½ cups button
mushrooms, wiped and
sliced
125g/4oz/heaping ½ cup
chick peas (garbanzo
beans), soaked, cooked and
drained
1tbsp chopped fresh parsley
sea salt
freshly ground black pepper
1 egg
150ml/5fl oz/⅔ cup milk or
single (light) cream
75g/3oz/¾ cup grated
cheese

Preheat the oven to 220°C/425°F/Gas 7. Roll out the pastry and line a 20cm/8 inch quiche dish; prick the base and bake in the oven for 15 minutes.

Make the filling by melting the butter in a saucepan and frying the onion and garlic for about 10 minutes, until tender but not browned. Add the mushrooms and cook for a further 3–4 minutes. Stir in the cooked chick peas (garbanzo beans) and the chopped parsley and season with sea salt and freshly ground black pepper. Put the mixture straight into the hot quiche case. Beat together the egg and milk or cream, season with sea salt and freshly ground black pepper, then pour into the quiche case. Scatter the grated cheese over the top. Bake the quiche in the preheated oven for 40–50 minutes until it's set and golden brown. As with the other quiches in this chapter, different beans can be used according to your inclination and storecupboard.

bean, pepper and tomato quiche

This is a very tasty quiche. Try it with a bowl of crisp mixed salad or with cooked green beans or buttery young carrots.

serves 6

Preheat the oven to 220°C/425°F/Gas 7. Roll out the pastry and line a 20cm/8 inch quiche dish. Prick the base and bake the quiche in the oven for about 15 minutes, until crisp. Reduce the heat to 180°C/350°F/Gas 4. Meanwhile, make the filling. Melt the butter in a medium-sized saucepan and fry the onion, garlic and green pepper for 10 minutes. Remove from the heat and add the tomatoes, basil and beans. Season with sea salt and freshly ground black pepper and pour this mixture into the hot quiche case.

Beat together the egg and milk or cream, season it with sea salt and freshly ground black pepper, then pour it carefully into the quiche case. Bake for 40–50 minutes, until set and golden. Serve hot or cold.

Of course, other types of beans can also be used for this quiche. Cannellini, butter or lima beans, flageolets and red kidney beans are all suitable.

1 quantity of shortcrust (pie) pastry – see page 162

For the filling
25g/1oz/2tbsp butter
1 onion, peeled and sliced
1 clove garlic, crushed
1 medium-sized sweet green pepper, deseeded and sliced
2 tomatoes, peeled and sliced
½tsp dried basil
125g/4oz/heaping ½ cup haricot (navy) beans, soaked, cooked and drained
sea salt
freshly ground black pepper
1 egg
150ml/5fl oz/⅔ cup milk or single (light) cream

lentil and green pepper quiche

The green pepper looks attractive in this quiche because it contrasts well with the colour of the lentils.

serves 6

1 quantity of shortcrust (pie) pastry – see page 162

For the filling
175g/6oz/scant 1 cup split red lentils
350ml/12fl oz/1½ cups water or vegetable stock
1 onion, peeled and chopped
1 clove garlic, crushed
25g/1oz/2tbsp butter
1 sweet green pepper
125g/4oz/1 cup grated cheese
1tbsp tomato paste
1 egg
sea salt
freshly ground black pepper

Set the oven to 220°C/425°F/Gas 7. Roll out the pastry and line a 20cm/8 inch quiche dish; prick the base and bake in the oven for 15 minutes, or until set and golden brown. Take it out of the oven and set aside. Turn the oven down to 180°C/350°F/Gas 4.

Wash and pick over the lentils, then put them into a saucepan with the water or stock and simmer gently under tender, 20–30 minutes. Fry the onion and garlic in the butter, without browning, for about 5 minutes. While that's happening, wash the green pepper and slice it into thin rings, discarding the seeds. Add it to the onion and garlic in the saucepan and cook for about 5 minutes, then add the onion and pepper mixture to the cooked lentils, together with the grated cheese, tomato paste and egg, and sea salt and freshly ground black pepper to taste. Spread the mixture in the prepared quiche case and bake in the oven for about 40 minutes.

lentil, tomato and mushroom quiche

This quiche is nice hot or cold; if you're serving it hot, try it with some parsley sauce.

serves 6

Preheat the oven to 220°C/425°F/Gas 7. Use the pastry to line a 20cm/8 inch quiche dish. Prick the base and bake the quiche in the oven for about 15 minutes, until the pastry is set, golden and crisp. Turn the oven down to 180°C/350°F/Gas 4.

Wash and pick over the lentils, then put them into a saucepan with the stock or water and cook until they're tender and have absorbed all the water, 20–30 minutes.

Fry the onion in the butter in a medium-sized saucepan for 10 minutes, but don't brown it, then add the mushrooms and cook for another 3–4 minutes. Stir in the cooked lentils, parsley, grated cheese, egg and plenty of seasoning. Spoon the mixture into the cooked quiche case and smooth the top. Slice the tomatoes and arrange them on the top of the quiche. Bake for about 40 minutes, watching it towards the end so that it doesn't get too dry.

1 quantity of shortcrust
(pie) pastry – see page 162

For the filling
175g/6oz /scant 1 cup split
red lentils
350ml/12fl oz/1½ cups
vegetable stock or water
1 large onion, peeled and
chopped
25g/1oz/2tbsp butter
125g/4oz/1½ cups
mushrooms, wiped and
sliced
1tbsp chopped fresh parsley
125g/4oz/1 cup grated
cheese
1 egg
sea salt
freshly ground black pepper
2 tomatoes

red bean and tomato quiche

The red beans, tomatoes and parsley make this a colourful quiche.

serves 6

1 quantity of shortcrust (pie) pastry – see page 162

For the filling
1 onion, peeled and chopped
1 clove garlic, crushed
2tbsp oil
3 tomatoes, peeled and chopped
125g/4oz/⅔ cup red kidney beans, soaked, cooked and drained
150ml/5fl oz/⅔ cup soured cream
1 egg
½tsp paprika
pinch of chilli powder
sea salt
freshly ground black pepper
1tbsp chopped fresh parsley

Preheat the oven to 220°C/425°F/Gas 7. Use the pastry to line a 20cm/8 inch quiche dish. Prick the base of the quiche and bake in the oven for 15 minutes, until set and crisp. Remove the quiche from the oven; turn the heat down to 180°C/350°F/Gas 4.

Next, make the filling. Fry the onion and garlic in the oil in a medium-sized saucepan for 10 minutes. Remove the saucepan from the heat and add the tomatoes and beans. You can mash the beans a little as you mix them in, or leave them whole, whichever you prefer. In a small bowl, beat together the soured cream and the egg, then stir them into the bean mixture, together with the paprika, a good pinch of chilli powder and sea salt and freshly ground black pepper to taste. Pour the mixture into the quiche case and sprinkle with the chopped parsley. Bake the quiche in the oven for 35–40 minutes, until set. It's lovely warm, with a green salad.

The Hindus have a saying: 'Rice is good, but lentils are my life', but I would add that if you put the two together you have the most potent combination of all. Actually this mixture of pulses (legumes) and rice happens naturally in dishes all over the world, from the dals and rice of India to the red beans and rice of the West Indies and the red rice of Japan. Certainly the two foods taste very good together, and their proteins complement each other, offering excellent nourishment. Many of these recipes use brown rice, but you could equally well use white if you prefer.

with rice and cereals

bean paella

Don't be put off by the rather long list of ingredients in this recipe; it's very easy to make and tastes delicious.

serves 4

125g/4oz/⅔ cup beans – red kidney beans look nice, or a mixture
225g/8oz/heaping 1 cup long grain brown rice
400ml/14fl oz/1¾ cups water
½tsp turmeric
sea salt
2tbsp oil
1 large onion, peeled and chopped
1 sweet green pepper, deseeded and chopped
1 celery stalk, chopped
2 large carrots, scraped and diced
1 small aubergine (eggplant), diced
1 large clove garlic, crushed
2 large tomatoes, peeled and chopped
125g/4oz/1½ cups button mushrooms, wiped and sliced
freshly ground black pepper
2tbsp chopped fresh parsley

Soak, drain and rinse the beans as usual. Cook them until tender – if using red kidney beans, boil them vigorously for the first 10 minutes. Meanwhile, wash the rice and put it into a large saucepan with the water, turmeric and sea salt to taste. Bring it up to the boil, then give it a stir, put a lid on the saucepan and turn down the heat. Let the rice cook gently for 30 minutes.

Heat the oil in a saucepan and fry the prepared onion, green pepper, celery, carrots, aubergine (eggplant) and garlic for 10 minutes, but don't let them brown. Add the tomatoes and mushrooms and cook for 5 minutes. Tip all this mixture on top of the rice. Drain the beans and put them on top of the rice and vegetables, then put a lid on the saucepan and let it all go on cooking over a low heat for a further 15 minutes. Then turn off the heat and leave the paella to stand for another 10 minutes. After this, stir the mixture carefully with a fork and add some sea salt and freshly ground black pepper to taste and the chopped parsley. Reheat gently if necessary before serving.

bean and wheat casserole

It's easy to get the crushed pre-cooked wheat called bulgur at supermarkets and health food stores, and it makes a pleasant casserole with beans and vegetables. Alternatively, you could use couscous.

serves 4

Soak, drain and rinse the beans as usual, then cover them with cold water and cook them gently until they're all tender, about 1 hour. Set the oven to 190°C/375°F/Gas 5.

Peel and chop the onion; deseed and chop the green pepper. Scrape and slice the carrots, crush the garlic and slice the celery. Then fry them all gently in the oil with the bayleaf for about 15 minutes, but don't let them brown. Remove the bayleaf. Add the bulgur wheat, tomatoes, tomato paste and seasonings to the mixture, together with the drained beans. Spoon the mixture into a greased shallow casserole dish and sprinkle with breadcrumbs. Dot a few small pieces of butter over the top, then bake for about 30 minutes. Serve with a quickly cooked green vegetable or a green salad.

350g/12oz/1½ cups mixed beans – I generally use a mixture of split red lentils, haricot (navy) beans and green lentils
1 large onion
1 large sweet green pepper
3 carrots
1 large clove garlic
3 celery stalks
3tbsp oil
1 bayleaf
150g/5oz/scant 1 cup bulgur wheat
400g/14oz can tomatoes
1tbsp tomato paste
½tsp chilli powder
sea salt
freshly ground black pepper

For the topping
a few dried breadcrumbs
a little butter

bean and vegetable curry

This is a mild curry with a lovely spicy flavour. I usually serve it with fried rice, but it's also good with plain boiled brown rice and some mango chutney. Lima beans can be used instead of butter beans; they will take 45–60 minutes to cook at the beginning.

serves 4

175g/6oz/scant 1 cup butter beans
3tbsp oil
1 onion, peeled and chopped
1 clove garlic, crushed
1tsp ground cumin
1tsp turmeric
¼tsp chilli powder
2 tomatoes, peeled and roughly chopped – you can used canned ones
450g/1lb potatoes, peeled and cut into chunky cubes
1½tsp sea salt
2 bayleaves
125g/4oz/scant 1 cup frozen peas

Soak, drain and rinse the beans as usual. Put the beans into a saucepan, cover them with their height again in cold water and let them simmer gently until they're tender, about 1¼ hours. Then drain the beans, reserving their liquor and making it up to 300ml/10fl oz/1¼ cups with extra water if necessary.

Heat the oil in a good-sized saucepan and add the onion and garlic. Fry them for 5 minutes, but don't brown them, then stir in the spices and cook for 1 minute before adding the tomatoes. Let them simmer together, with a lid on the saucepan, for about 5 minutes, then add the potatoes and mix well so that they are coated with the spice mixture. Stir in the reserved 300ml/10fl oz/1¼ cups of liquid and the sea salt and bayleaves. Put a lid on the saucepan and let everything simmer gently until the potatoes are nearly cooked, then add the beans and peas and cook for a further 5–6 minutes.

curried chick peas

serves 3–4

Soak, drain and rinse the chick peas (garbanzo beans) as usual. Put them into a saucepan with plenty of cold water and simmer them gently for 1½–3 hours, until they're tender. Drain off and reserve the cooking liquid.

Heat the oil in a medium-sized saucepan and fry the cumin seeds for 1 minute, then add the onion, ginger, turmeric, ground cumin, ground coriander and garam masala and fry for 2 minutes, stirring all the time. Mix in the cooked chick peas (garbanzo beans) and then 300ml/10fl oz/1¼ cups of the reserved cooking liquid and bring to the boil. Put a lid on the saucepan and let everything simmer gently for 10–15 minutes. Season to taste and sprinkle with the chopped coriander (cilantro). Serve with rice.

225g/8oz/heaping 1 cup chick peas (garbanzo beans)
3tbsp vegetable oil
1tsp cumin seeds
1 small onion, finely chopped
½tsp ground ginger
½tsp turmeric
½tsp ground cumin
½tsp ground coriander
½tsp garam masala
sea salt
2tbsp chopped fresh coriander (cilantro)

curried lentil and pineapple

Many of the pulses (legumes) are enhanced by being served with something sweet, and I particularly like this English-style curry which is a mixture of split red lentils and pineapple. Serve it with rice and lime pickle.

serves 4

1 large onion
1 clove garlic
2tbsp oil
4tsp curry powder
350g/12oz/1¾ cups split red lentils
400g/14oz can pineapple pieces
900ml/1½ pints/3¾ cups water
sea salt
freshly ground black pepper

To serve
a little desiccated (dried shredded) coconut
1 tomato, sliced

Peel and finely chop the onion; crush the garlic. Fry them together in the oil in a large saucepan for 10 minutes, then mix in the curry powder and lentils and stir for a minute or two so that they get well coated with the oil and curry powder. Drain and roughly mash the pineapple and add it to the saucepan, together with the water. Bring the mixture up to the boil, then cover the saucepan with a lid and cook over a gentle heat for 20–30 minutes, until the lentils are soft. Season with sea salt and freshly ground black pepper. Pile on a warm serving dish, sprinkle with the coconut and garnish with the sliced tomato.

curried mung dal

Whether or not you soak the mung beans is up to you; they cook quickly in any case.

serves 4

Soak, drain and rinse the mung beans. Cover them with cold water and cook in the usual way until tender, 20–30 minutes. Or cook the beans without soaking, in which case they will take around 30–40 minutes to soften. Drain off any extra water.

Heat the oil in a medium-sized saucepan and fry the onion and garlic for 10 minutes, then add the cumin, turmeric and chilli powder and cook for 2–3 minutes. Stir in the drained mung beans and season well with sea salt and freshly ground black pepper. Cook the mixture over a low heat, stirring all the time, until everything is well blended and piping hot. Serve with cooked rice and a salad.

350g/12oz/1¾ cups mung beans
4tbsp oil
1 large onion, peeled and chopped
1 large clove garlic, crushed
1½tsp ground cumin
1½tsp turmeric
¼–½tsp chilli powder
sea salt
freshly ground black pepper

curried red kidney beans

Red kidney beans make a superb curry. Serve with plain boiled rice and chutney.

serves 4

225g/8oz/1⅓ cups red kidney beans, soaked, drained and rinsed
1 medium-sized onion
1 large clove garlic
1½tbsp vegetable oil
1–2tsp grated fresh ginger
2tsp ground coriander
1tsp turmeric
½tsp ground cumin
½tsp garam masala
2 large tomatoes, peeled and chopped – you can use canned ones
sea salt
chopped fresh coriander (cilantro)

Cover the beans with plenty of cold water and bring to the boil. Boil vigorously for 10 minutes, then lower the heat and cook gently for about 1 hour, or until tender.

Peel and chop the onion and crush the garlic. Fry them in the oil in a largish saucepan, together with the grated ginger, for 6-7 minutes, stirring them from time to time. Add the ground coriander, turmeric and garam masala and cook for a further minute or two, stirring, before adding the tomatoes. Then put a lid on the saucepan and let everything cook gently for 5 minutes.

Drain the cooked beans, reserving 150ml/5fl oz/⅔ cup of the liquid. Add this liquid to the tomato and spice mixture, together with a good teaspoon of sea salt. Let it simmer for a further 5 minutes, then add the drained beans and heat them through. Serve hot, sprinkled with chopped coriander (cilantro).

dal

As the split red lentils used in this recipe cook in half an hour without soaking, this dish is quickly made. In fact if you want to serve it with brown rice, it's best to get the rice cooking before you start making the dal.

serves 3–4

Put the lentils, water and bayleaf into a saucepan and cook gently for about 30 minutes, until the lentils are tender and have absorbed all the water.

Meanwhile, heat the oil in a saucepan and fry the onion and garlic with the turmeric, cumin, coriander and ginger for 10 minutes, stirring from time to time. Add the tomatoes and cook for a further minute or two before putting in the carrot, green pepper and leek. Mix well, so that all the vegetables are coated with the spices, then put a lid on the saucepan and turn down the heat. Cook gently for about 15 minutes or until the vegetables are all tender. Stir the vegetables into the cooked lentils and season with sea salt and freshly ground black pepper. Serve with plain boiled or fried rice.

225g/8oz/heaping 1 cup split red lentils
400ml/14fl oz/1¾ cups water
1 bayleaf
3tbsp oil
1 large onion, peeled and chopped
1 clove garlic, crushed
1tsp turmeric
1tsp ground cumin
1tsp ground coriander
1tsp grated fresh ginger
2 tomatoes, peeled and chopped
1 large carrot, scraped and diced
1 large sweet green pepper, deseeded and sliced
1 leek, washed and sliced
sea salt
freshly ground black pepper

japanese red-cooked rice

Sekihan, as this dish is called, is known as a 'happy food' in Japan because it turns out a pinkish red and the Japanese consider that colour to be lucky and joyous. For this reason it is traditional to serve sekihan at festivals and, in particular, at weddings.

If you wanted to be really authentic you'd use a Japanese rice for this recipe. I find a short grain brown rice is quite satisfactory, although of course the red colouring is not quite so intense.

You need to start this dish at least a day before you plan to eat it.

serves 3–4

125g/4oz/heaping ½ cup adzuki beans
225g/8oz/heaping 1 cup short grain brown rice
sea salt
1–2tsp black sesame seeds

Wash the adzuki beans, put them into a saucepan and cover them with 1.2 litres/2 pints/1¼ quarts water. Simmer the beans for about 40–45 minutes, until they're tender, then drain them well, reserving the liquid.

Wash and pick over the rice; put it into a bowl and pour in the reserved bean liquid. Leave in a cool place to soak overnight.

Next day, drain the rice and discard the liquid. Mix the cooked adzuki beans with the rice, also a little sea salt, and place them in the top of a steamer. Steam gently for 40–60 minutes, until the rice is tender.

Heat the sesame seeds in a dry frying pan for 2–3 minutes, until they're lightly toasted, then mix them with ½tsp sea salt. Serve the rice sprinkled with the sesame seeds and hand round soy sauce (preferably Japanese). A crunchy green salad, with a flavoursome, slightly sweet dressing, goes well with this.

khitchari

Khitchari is a mixture of rice and mung beans. The name actually means 'mess', as in 'mess of pottage', and is the origin of kedgeree. It's a deliciously spicy mixture and the only accompaniment it needs is some mango chutney and perhaps a side salad of sliced tomato and raw onion rings.

serves 3–4

Wash and pick over the beans and the rice. Peel and chop the onion and fry it in the oil in a medium-sized saucepan for 5 minutes. Add the garlic, turmeric, ginger, cumin and chilli powder and fry for a further 3–4 minutes, stirring from time to time. Quarter two of the tomatoes, reserving the other for garnish, and add to the saucepan, together with the potato, mung beans and rice. Fry over a gentle heat for 5 minutes, then stir in the water and bring the mixture up to the boil. Cover the saucepan, turn down the heat and cook very gently for about 45 minutes, until the rice and beans are cooked.

Turn off the heat and leave the saucepan to stand, covered, for a further 10–15 minutes, by which time all the liquid should have been absorbed. Add the lemon juice and garam masala, and sea salt to taste, stirring gently with a fork to avoid mashing the rice. Serve garnished with the remaining tomato, cut into rings.

If you want to make a spicier version, add a few cardamom pods, 4 or 5 cloves, or a small piece of cinnamon stick with the other spices.

225g/8oz/heaping 1 cup mung beans
225g/8oz/heaping 1 cup long grain brown rice
1 large onion
3tbsp oil
4 cloves garlic, crushed
½tsp turmeric
1tsp grated fresh ginger
1tsp ground cumin
pinch of chilli powder
3 tomatoes, peeled
1 large potato, peeled and cut into chunky pieces
900ml/1½ pints/3¾ cups water
2tbsp lemon juice
½tsp garam masala
sea salt

quick lentil curry

This is a simple, English-style curry. Serve it with some rice and mango chutney.

serves 4

2 onions, peeled and chopped
1 apple, peeled and chopped
3tbsp oil
1 bayleaf
1 large clove garlic, crushed
1–1½tbsp curry powder
350g/12oz/1¾ cups split red lentils, washed but not soaked
900ml/1½ pints/3¾ cups water
sea salt
freshly ground black pepper
a little lemon juice to taste

Fry the onions and apple in the oil in a medium-sized saucepan for 5 minutes, then add the bayleaf, garlic and curry powder and continue to cook for 3–4 minutes. Stir in the lentils and mix them round so that they get coated in the oil and curry powder, then add the water and bring the mixture up to the boil. Put a lid on the saucepan, turn the heat down and simmer gently for about 30 minutes, or until the lentils are cooked. Season with sea salt, freshly ground black pepper and lemon juice; remove the bayleaf before serving.

rice with chick peas and tomatoes

This rice dish is good hot or cold and it's full of protein. I think it's worth using olive oil if possible, because of the flavour.

serves 4

Soak and cook the chick peas (garbanzo beans) as usual, then drain them and mash lightly to break them up a little. Wash the rice carefully, then put it into a medium-sized saucepan with the water and 1tsp sea salt. Bring up to the boil, then put a lid on the saucepan and leave to simmer very gently for 45 minutes to cook the rice.

Meanwhile, peel and finely chop the onions and fry them in the olive oil in a large saucepan until they're soft but not browned, 10 minutes. Add the garlic, chick peas (garbanzo beans) and tomatoes and cook for a further few minutes to make everything nice and hot, then stir in the cooked rice and the chopped parsley and lemon juice, using a fork so that you don't mash the rice. Add more sea salt to taste and a good grinding of black pepper. Serve immediately, or let the mixture cool and then serve it as part of a salad meal.

350g/12oz/1¾ cups chick peas (garbanzo beans)
225g/8oz/heaping 1 cup long grain brown rice
400ml/14fl oz/1¾ cups water
sea salt
2 large onions
6tbsp olive oil
4 cloves garlic, crushed
450g/1lb tomatoes, peeled and sliced
2–3tbsp chopped fresh parsley
2tbsp lemon juice
freshly ground black pepper

rice and peas

The 'peas' in this dish are actually red kidney beans, but this recipe was given to me by a friend who lives in the Caribbean, and I've kept the original name. She tells me it's a popular dish out there and they generally use immature or 'water coconuts', as they call them, for the coconut milk. We can use canned coconut milk.

serves 4

2tbsp oil
1 medium onion, peeled and chopped
1 sweet red pepper, deseeded and chopped
350g/12oz/heaping 1½ cups long grain brown rice
400g/14oz can coconut milk
½tsp dried thyme
sea salt
freshly ground black pepper
300ml/10fl oz/1¼ cups cold water
175g/6oz/1 cup red kidney beans, soaked, cooked and drained as usual

Heat the oil in a large saucepan and fry the onion until golden. Add the red pepper, rice, coconut milk, thyme, sea salt, freshly ground black pepper and water and bring up to the boil. Cover the saucepan, turn the heat right down and leave to cook very slowly for 45 minutes, until the rice is tender and all the liquid absorbed.

Stir in the cooked red beans, using a fork so that you don't mash the rice, and cook for a further few minutes to heat the beans through. Serve with a nice crisp green salad with a herby dressing.

simple curried lentils

This spicy lentil mixture is lovely with plain boiled rice and a tomato and onion or cucumber and yogurt side salad.

serves 3

If possible, soak the lentils for a few hours in cold water. Rinse them, then put them into a saucepan with water just to cover. Simmer for about 40 minutes, or until they're tender. If there isn't time to soak them, either do the quick, hot soak – see page xxii –and then cook them, or put the washed lentils into a saucepan with plenty of water and simmer them for about 1–1¼ hours or so until they're tender. In any case, drain the lentils well.

Fry the onions and garlic in the butter for about 5 minutes, then add the ground coriander and cumin and cook for a further 5 minutes. Stir the onion and spices into the cooked lentils and flavour with the lemon juice, sea salt and freshly ground black pepper.

That's the basic, simple curry, but you can jazz it up by adding other vegetables, such as sliced sweet green pepper or button mushrooms – fry them with the onions.

225g/8oz/heaping 1 cup green lentils

2 large onions, peeled and chopped

2 cloves garlic, crushed

50g/2oz/¼ cup butter

2tsp ground coriander

2tsp ground cumin

juice of ½ lemon

sea salt

freshly ground black pepper

soya bean curry

You need to allow time for the beans to soak and cook, so it's a good idea to get started on this recipe a day or two before you plan to make it – or use canned ones.

serves 4

175g/6oz/1 cup soya beans
(soybeans)
1 large onion
1 clove garlic
1 sweet apple
2tbsp oil
2–3tsp curry powder
2tbsp plain (all-purpose)
flour
400ml/14fl oz/1¾ cups
water
125g/4oz/scant 1 cup
sultanas (golden raisins)
sea salt
freshly ground black pepper
lemon juice
a little sugar

Wash the beans, cover them with plenty of cold water and leave them to soak for 12 hours. Drain and rinse them thoroughly and put them into a saucepan with a good covering of water. Cook them gently until they're very tender – this takes about 3–4 hours. Drain the beans.

Peel and chop the onion and crush the garlic. Peel, core and chop the apple. Fry them in the oil for 10 minutes, without browning, then stir in the curry powder and flour and cook for a minute or two longer. Pour in the water and stir until thickened, then add the sultanas (golden raisins) and the beans and simmer gently, covered, for 15 minutes. Season with sea salt and freshly ground black pepper and add a little lemon juice. If necessary, add a little sugar to taste.

This is good served with plain boiled rice and some mango chutney.

split pea dal with hardboiled eggs

This is a pretty dish – yellow split pea dal against white and yellow hardboiled eggs with a fresh green garnish. It's nice with plain fluffy rice.

serves 4

Soak, drain and rinse the split peas as usual, then cook them in fresh cold water until they're tender. Drain off any excess liquid.

Meanwhile, heat the vegetable oil in a good-sized saucepan and fry the onions and garlic for 5 minutes, then add the ground cumin and turmeric and fry for a further 5 minutes. Mix in the cooked split peas and heat gently, stirring often to prevent sticking. When it's piping hot, add the lemon juice, and sea salt and freshly ground black pepper to taste. Serve it heaped up on a warm serving dish with the hardboiled egg quarters round the edge and the coriander (cilantro) sprinkled on top.

225g/8oz/1 cup yellow split peas
4tbsp vegetable oil
2 large onions, peeled and chopped
2 large cloves garlic, crushed
3tsp ground cumin
3tsp turmeric
1tbsp lemon juice
sea salt
freshly ground black pepper
4 hardboiled eggs, cut into quarters
1–2tbsp chopped fresh coriander (cilantro)

west indian red beans

The creamed coconut in this recipe gives the touch of sweetness so characteristic of Caribbean cookery. It also thickens the sauce. It's available in blocks from health food stores and supermarkets.

Incidentally, this dish is always very strongly seasoned with thyme, but if you think the amount given will be too powerful, start with less. West Indian red beans are nice served with lots of plain boiled rice.

serves 4

225g/8oz/1⅓ cups red kidney beans
1 large onion, peeled and sliced
1 large carrot, scraped and sliced
1 large clove garlic, crushed
1tbsp dried thyme
75g/3oz creamed coconut
sea salt
freshly ground black pepper

Soak, drain and rinse the beans as usual. Put the beans, onion, carrot and garlic into a large saucepan and cover them with cold water. Boil vigorously for 10 minutes, then lower the heat and simmer gently for 45 minutes, until the beans are nearly cooked. Add the thyme and continue cooking for another 15–30 minutes to finish cooking the beans. Cut the creamed coconut into pieces and add to the bean mixture; heat gently, stirring occasionally, until all the coconut has melted. Season carefully with sea salt and freshly ground black pepper.

I'm particularly fond of stuffed vegetables because it's possible to make them look so colourful and attractive. And although many of these dishes are really quite cheap, they always look special.

You may feel that these stuffed vegetable are rather time-consuming and fiddly to prepare but, as with most pulse (legume) cookery, they're done in simple stages and it's largely a question of organization.

The stuffings all freeze well, so it's worthwhile making up an extra amount and freezing it ready for another occasion.

stuffed vegetables

aubergines stuffed with chick peas

Aubergines, or eggplants as they are known in the US, stuffed with chick peas make a lovely dish, reminiscent of the Middle East. It's good served cold, as well as hot.

serves 4

2 medium-sized aubergines (eggplants)
sea salt
oil for frying

For the stuffing
1 large onion, peeled and sliced
1 large clove garlic, crushed
3 large tomatoes, peeled and chopped
175g/6oz/scant 1 cup chick peas (garbanzo beans), soaked, cooked and drained
2–3tsp lemon juice
2 good tbsp chopped fresh parsley
freshly ground black pepper

Cut the aubergines (eggplants) in half and scoop out the insides. Sprinkle the insides of the skins and the scooped-out flesh with sea salt and set aside for about 30 minutes for the bitter juices to be drawn out. Then wash the skins and scooped-out flesh and pat dry.

Set the oven to 180°C/350°F/Gas 4. Put a little oil in the base of a frying pan and fry the skins on both sides to soften them a little, then place them in an oiled shallow casserole dish. Fry the onion, garlic and scooped-out flesh in 3tbsp oil in a large saucepan until they're tender – about 10 minutes – then add the tomatoes and cook for a further 2–3 minutes. Remove from the heat and add the cooked chick peas (garbanzo beans), lemon juice and parsley, and sea salt and freshly ground black pepper to taste. Divide the mixture between the aubergine (eggplant) skins, piling it up well. Bake in the oven for 30–40 minutes. They're nice with creamy mashed potatoes and a cooked green vegetable.

aubergines stuffed with lentils and mushrooms

Aubergines – eggplants as they are known in the US – are superb with a stuffing of lentils and mushrooms.

serves 4

Prepare the aubergines (eggplants) as described in the previous recipe – salting them, then frying the skins in oil. Arrange the skins in a shallow casserole dish.

Set the oven to 180°C/350°F/Gas 4. Fry the onion, garlic and scooped-out aubergine (eggplant) flesh in 3tbsp oil in a good-sized saucepan for about 10 minutes, until the onion is soft, then add the mushrooms and cook for a further 4–5 minutes. Mix in the cooked lentils, lemon juice and parsley, and some sea salt and freshly ground black pepper to taste. Pile the mixture into the aubergine (eggplant) skins and sprinkle with some crumbs and grated cheese. Bake them in the oven for 30–40 minutes, until the skins are completely cooked and the topping is a nice golden brown.

2 medium-sized aubergines (eggplants)
sea salt
oil for frying

For the stuffing
1 large onion, peeled and chopped
2 cloves garlic, crushed
125g/4oz/1½ cups button mushrooms, wiped and sliced
125g/4oz/heaping ½ cup green lentils, soaked and cooked as usual
1–2tsp lemon juice
2tbsp chopped fresh parsley
freshly ground black pepper

To finish
dried crumbs
a little grated cheese

courgettes with chick pea and mushroom stuffing

Courgettes, or zucchini as they are known in the US, are delicious stuffed with chick peas (garbanzo beans). The firm texture of the chick peas (garbanzo beans) contrasts well with the tender courgette (zucchini) and mushrooms.

serves 4

4 good-sized courgettes (zucchini), about 750g/1½lb

For the stuffing
50g/2oz/¼ cup butter
1 onion, peeled and chopped
2 cloves garlic, crushed
125g/4oz/1½ cups button mushrooms, wiped and sliced
1–2tsp ground coriander
125g/4oz/heaping ½ cup chick peas (garbanzo beans), soaked and cooked as usual
juice of ½ lemon
2tbsp chopped fresh coriander (cilantro)
sea salt
freshly ground black pepper

Set the oven to 180°C/350°F/Gas 4. Wash the courgettes (zucchini), then cut them in half lengthwise and scoop out the insides, leaving a shell. Arrange these in a buttered shallow casserole dish. Chop up the scooped-out flesh. Melt the butter in a saucepan and fry the onion and garlic for 5 minutes, then add the chopped flesh and the sliced mushrooms and cook for a further 5 minutes. Mix in the ground coriander, the cooked and drained chick peas (garbanzo beans), lemon juice and fresh coriander (cilantro). Season with sea salt and freshly ground black pepper and pile the mixture into the shells. Bake in the oven for 30–40 minutes, until the courgettes (zucchini) are tender. They're nice served hot with a tomato sauce and some French (fine green) beans, or chilled Middle Eastern style and served with plain yogurt.

stuffed mushroom caps

Large, flat mushrooms make a very good base for a tasty lentil stuffing and look appetizing when garnished with lemon and parsley. If you serve the mushrooms on circles of fried bread, it makes them more substantial, as well as giving a pleasantly crisp texture. If you cut the circles for the fried bread first, the excess bread can be made into crumbs for the stuffing.

serves 3-6

Set the oven to 180°C/350°F/Gas 4. Wash the mushrooms and trim off any stems level with the base. Chop up the stems. Cover the base of a large saucepan with a thin layer of oil and heat it up. Fry the mushroom caps for a minute or two on each side, then remove them from the saucepan and put them on one side.

Put a little more oil in the saucepan – there should be about 6tbsp in all – and fry the onion, garlic and chopped mushroom stems for 10 minutes, letting them brown lightly. Then mix in the breadcrumbs and stir until they're brown and crunchy. Remove from the heat and add the cooked and well drained lentils, thyme, parsley, lemon rind and enough juice to give a pleasant flavour. Season well.

Cut the slices of bread into circles to fit the mushroom caps. Fry the bread on both sides in a little oil until crisp. Arrange the bread circles on a flat ovenproof plate or baking tray and place a mushroom cap, black side up, on each. Divide the stuffing mixture between the mushroom caps, piling it up neatly. Bake in the oven for about 20 minutes to heat them through. Garnish each with a slice of lemon and a sprig of parsley before serving. They go well with very light, creamy mashed potatoes, French (fine green) beans, and grilled tomatoes.

12 large, flat mushrooms
oil for frying

For the stuffing
175g/6oz/scant 1 cup green lentils, soaked and cooked as usual
1 large onion, peeled and chopped
1 large clove garlic, crushed
175g/6oz/3 cups whole-wheat breadcrumbs
1tsp dried thyme
1tbsp chopped fresh parsley
grated rind and juice of ½ lemon
sea salt
freshly ground black pepper
12 slices of wholewheat bread
12 slices of lemon
12 sprigs of parsley

stuffed onions

This is a warming, winter dish. It goes well with Bircher potatoes, which you can cook in the oven at the same time as the onions. To make these, simply scrub some medium-sized old potatoes, halve them lengthwise and put them, cut side down, on an oiled baking sheet. Sprinkle them with sea salt, and a few caraway seeds if you like them, and bake the potatoes at the top of the oven while the onions cook in the middle.

serves 4

4 large onions

For the stuffing
75g/3oz/scant ½ cup green lentils, soaked and cooked as usual
1 clove garlic, crushed
2tsp tomato paste
125g/4oz/1 cup grated cheese
½tsp dried thyme
sea salt
freshly ground black pepper

Peel the onions and cook them for 15 minutes in boiling salted water; drain and cool. Preheat the oven to 200°C/400°F/Gas 6. With a sharp knife, scoop out the insides of the onions, leaving the outer layers intact. Chop up the scooped-out onion and mix it with the cooked and drained lentils, the garlic, tomato paste, cheese and thyme. Season with sea salt and freshly ground black pepper. Divide the mixture between the onions, pushing it well down into the cavities. Put the onions into an oiled casserole dish and, if there's any of the stuffing mixture leftover, scatter that round the onions. Bake them in the preheated oven for 30–40 minutes.

stuffed sweet peppers

These are always popular. In this recipe I've suggested four medium-sized peppers, but you could use two large ones split in half.

serves 4

Soak, drain and rinse the red kidney beans as usual. Put them into a heavy-based saucepan with the water and boil vigorously for 10 minutes. Add the brown rice, then turn the heat down. Leave them to simmer gently, with a lid on the saucepan, for 45 minutes, until the rice and beans are both cooked and all the water has been absorbed.

Set the oven to 190°C/375°F/Gas 5. Prepare the peppers by slicing off their stem ends and removing the seeds, then put them into a large saucepan of boiling water and simmer them gently for 2–3 minutes. Drain them well and pat them dry with paper towels. Place the peppers in a greased shallow casserole dish and set aside while you make the filling.

Fry the onion and garlic in the oil for 5 minutes, then add the tomatoes, the cooked rice and beans, the walnuts and chilli powder, sea salt and freshly ground black pepper to taste. Spoon the filling into the peppers and replace the sliced-off tops as lids. Bake in the oven for 35–40 minutes, or until the peppers are completely tender. Serve them with a tomato sauce and some vegetables.

4 medium-sized sweet red or green peppers

For the stuffing
125g/4oz/⅔ cup red kidney beans
300ml/10fl oz/1¼ cups water
75g/3oz/scant ½ cup long grain brown rice, washed
1 large onion, peeled and chopped
1 large clove garlic, crushed
2tbsp oil
2 tomatoes, peeled and chopped
50g/2oz/½ cup walnuts, chopped
¼–½tsp chilli powder
sea salt
freshly ground black pepper

sweet peppers with lentil and tomato stuffing

This is a tasty dish, good with creamy potatoes and buttered baby carrots.

serves 4

4 medium-sized sweet green peppers
sea salt

For the stuffing
1 large onion
2 cloves garlic
3tbsp oil
1 bayleaf
6 tomatoes, peeled and chopped, or a 400g/14oz can, well drained
175g/6oz/scant 1 cup green lentils, soaked, cooked and drained
125g/4oz/2 cups whole-wheat breadcrumbs
2tbsp chopped fresh parsley
freshly ground black pepper

To finish
a little grated cheese

Preheat the oven to 180°C/350°F/Gas 4. Slice the tops off the green peppers and remove the seeds. Rinse the peppers inside and out under cold water, then put them into a large saucepan of boiling salted water and simmer them for 2–3 minutes. Drain and dry them and place them in a greased shallow casserole dish.

Peel and slice the onion and crush the garlic. Fry them together in the oil with the bayleaf for 10 minutes, then remove the bayleaf and stir in the tomatoes, cooked lentils, wholewheat breadcrumbs, parsley and a good seasoning of freshly ground black pepper and sea salt. Mix it all together well, then divide between the four peppers, piling it up well. Sprinkle the tops with grated cheese and bake in the oven for 30–40 minutes, or until the peppers are tender.

hot stuffed tomatoes

Serve on crisp circles of fried bread as a first course, or with rice or buttered noodles and a green vegetable or salad for a main meal.

serves 8 as a first course or 4 as a main dish

Cut a small slice from the top of each tomato, then, using a teaspoon, carefully scoop out the insides – these will not be needed in this recipe but can be used in tomato soups and sauces, etc. Sprinkle the insides of the tomatoes with a little sea salt; place the tomatoes upside down on a plate and leave for 30 minutes to draw out any excess liquid.

Preheat the oven to 180°C/350°F/Gas 4. Fry the onions and garlic in 3tbsp of the olive oil in a medium-sized saucepan for 10 minutes, until soft but not browned, then mix in the cooked chick peas (garbanzo beans), mashing them a bit as you do so. Add the basil, some sea salt and freshly ground black pepper and the lemon juice.

Use a little of the remaining olive oil to grease a shallow ovenproof dish. Place the tomatoes in the dish and fill each with some of the chick pea (garbanzo bean) mixture, piling it up well. Put any remaining mixture around the edges of the dish. Replace the sliced-off tomato tops as lids. Pour the remaining oil over the tomatoes and bake in the oven for 30–40 minutes. Serve them from the dish, garnished with some fresh parsley sprigs. Or, if serving them as a first course, place each tomato on a circle of crisp fried bread and serve on individual plates.

8 large tomatoes
sea salt

For the stuffing
2 large onions, peeled and chopped
3 cloves garlic, crushed
8tbsp olive oil
350g/12oz/1¾ cups chick peas (garbanzo beans), soaked, cooked and drained
2tsp dried basil
freshly ground black pepper
2tbsp lemon juice

To serve
fresh parsley sprigs
8 circles of fried bread, if serving the tomatoes as a first course

cold stuffed tomatoes

Flageolet beans make an attractive filling for stuffed tomatoes, their pale green colour contrasting well with the red.

serves 4

4 large, firm tomatoes
sea salt

For the stuffing
125g/4oz/heaping ½ cup
flageolet beans
4tbsp mayonnaise
1tbsp chopped fresh chives
1tbsp chopped fresh parsley
freshly ground black pepper
1–2 drops Tabasco

To serve
a few crisp lettuce leaves
parsley sprigs

Soak, drain, rinse and cook the beans as usual; drain well and mash them roughly.

Halve the tomatoes and scoop out their centres – these will not be needed for this recipe. Sprinkle the insides of the tomatoes with sea salt and then put them upside down on a plate to drain off any excess liquid.

Mix together the beans, mayonnaise, chives and parsley. Season with sea salt and freshly ground black pepper and one or two drops of Tabasco. Fill the tomato cavities with the bean mixture and chill. To serve, place the tomatoes on a base of crisp lettuce leaves and garnish with parsley.

A motley selection of dishes, mostly vegetable stews, all of which are quick to make, especially if you use canned beans, or dried beans which you've cooked and frozen. See page vi for freezing and comparative quantities of dried and canned pulses.

top-of-the-stove dishes

bean ratatouille

The addition of some beans to ratatouille turns this delectable dish into a main meal. If you use rather bland beans, such as haricots (navy) beans or cannellini, they will soak up the lovely flavour of the olive oil and garlic.

serves 4

175g/6oz/scant 1 cup haricot (navy) beans
2 large onions, peeled and chopped
3tbsp olive oil
3tbsp vegetable oil
3 large cloves garlic, crushed
2 sweet red peppers, deseeded and chopped
450g/1lb courgettes (zucchini), diced
450g/1lb aubergines (eggplants), diced
4 tomatoes, peeled and chopped – you can use canned ones
sea salt
freshly ground black pepper
a little chopped fresh parsley

Soak, rinse and cook the beans as usual until they're tender, then drain them.

Fry the onions in the oils in a large saucepan for about 10 minutes, then add the garlic, red peppers, courgettes (zucchini) and aubergines (eggplants). Cook gently with a lid on the saucepan for about 30 minutes, then add the tomatoes and cook for a further 30 minutes. Then stir in the beans and allow them to heat through. Season the mixture with sea salt and freshly ground black pepper and sprinkle it with parsley just before serving.

I like this with hot garlic bread, which, of course, supplies cereal protein to complement the beans and provide first-class nourishment. With a green salad fragrant with fresh herbs, and a glass of wine, bean ratatouille makes a lovely summer supper.

beans with marrow and corn

For this Latin American dish you can use any white beans. I like it with black eyed beans (peas), but haricot (navy) beans or cannellini are also good. Choose, if possible, a marrow that's tender enough for the skin to be left on, as the stripey green looks attractive against the red tomato and yellow sweetcorn. Pumpkin is very popular in south American cookery, and can be used instead of the marrow.

serves 4

Heat the oil in a good-sized saucepan and fry the onion for 5 minutes, until beginning to soften. Add the garlic, tomatoes, basil and oregano, and cook fairly fast for about 10 minutes, without a lid on the saucepan, to make a thickish sauce. Stir in the drained beans and marrow and simmer gently for about 10 minutes, until the marrow is nearly cooked, then mix in the sweetcorn and continue to cook until everything is tender and the mixture piping hot. Season with sea salt and freshly ground black pepper and serve at once.

3tbsp olive oil
1 large onion, peeled and chopped
1 large clove garlic, crushed
400g/14oz can tomatoes
1tsp dried basil
1tsp dried oregano
225g/8oz/1⅓ cups black eyed beans (peas), soaked, drained and cooked until very nearly tender
450g/1lb marrow (vegetable marrow), cut into largish dice
125g/4oz/heaping ½ cup sweetcorn kernels
sea salt
freshly ground black pepper

beany goulash

Strictly speaking, a genuine Hungarian *gulyas* or 'goulash' doesn't contain soured cream –
but then neither would it be made from beans. If you want the best flavoured paprika it's
well worth looking out for a Hungarian one, and buying only a small quantity at a time.

serves 4

225g/8oz/heaping 1 cup
cannellini or haricot (navy)
beans
4 cloves garlic, crushed
450g/1lb onions, peeled and
sliced
4tbsp oil
2 large sweet green
peppers, deseeded and
sliced
2 x 400g/14oz cans
tomatoes
4tbsp tomato paste
2–4tsp paprika
sea salt
freshly ground black pepper
a little sugar

To serve
150ml/5fl oz/⅔ cup soured
cream, if liked

Soak, drain and rinse the beans as usual, then simmer
them in fresh water for about 1 hour, until they're tender.

Fry the garlic and onions in the oil in a large saucepan
for about 10 minutes, until the onions are soft, then add
the green pepper and fry for a further 4–5 minutes. Mix in
the tomatoes, tomato paste and the drained beans, then
paprika, sea salt, freshly ground black pepper and perhaps
a little sugar to taste. Simmer the mixture for about 15
minutes, without a lid on the saucepan, to make everything
nice and hot and to reduce the liquid a little. Serve with
the soured cream if liked.

beorijch

An unusual mixture of black eyed beans (peas) and nuts, this is an Armenian dish that's rich in protein and quick to make. It's also very tasty.

serves 4

Soak, drain, rinse and cook the black eyed beans (peas) as usual; drain them well. Fry the onion in the olive oil in a good-sized saucepan for 10 minutes, then stir in the garlic, tomatoes and tomato paste and cook for a further 10 minutes to make a thick purée. Add the nuts, parsley and the beans, mashing them slightly as you do so. Taste the mixture and season with sea salt, freshly ground black pepper and a little sugar if you think it's necessary. Put over a gentle heat for about 10 minutes, stirring often to prevent sticking. Serve piping hot, with buttered new potatoes or creamy mashed potatoes and a cooked green vegetable or crisp green salad.

225g/8oz/1⅓ cups black eyed beans (peas)
1 large onion, peeled and chopped
4tbsp olive oil
1 clove garlic, crushed
2 tomatoes, peeled and chopped – you can use canned ones
1tbsp tomato paste
125g/4oz/1 cup mixed nuts, roughly chopped in the food processor or blender
2tbsp chopped fresh parsley
sea salt
freshly ground black pepper
a little sugar

black eyed bean and vegetable stew

This is a colourful stew, with black eyed beans (peas) peeping out of a rich red tomato sauce and a garnish of fresh green parsley. It goes well with couscous.

serves 4

225g/8oz/1⅓ cups black eyed beans (peas)
1 large onion
3 celery stalks
3 carrots
1 sweet green pepper
2 cloves garlic
50g/2oz/¼ cup butter
400g/14oz can tomatoes
1tbsp tomato paste
2–3tbsp red wine – if possible
sea salt
freshly ground black pepper
2tbsp chopped fresh parsley

Soak, drain and rinse the black eyed beans (peas) as usual. Put them into a saucepan, cover with cold water and simmer gently until tender, about 40 minutes. Drain the beans.

Peel and chop the onion. Slice the celery thinly and scrape and dice the carrots. Remove the seeds from the green pepper, then slice it fairly thinly; crush the garlic. Melt the butter in a good-sized saucepan and add all the prepared vegetables. Fry them gently, without browning, for about 10 minutes, then mix in the beans, tomatoes, tomato paste and the wine if you're using it. Season the mixture with sea salt and freshly ground black pepper and let it cook gently for 10–15 minutes, until all the vegetables are tender. Check seasoning. Serve sprinkled with the parsley.

bean and vegetable gratin

I tend to think of this as a winter dish, made with root vegetables, but in fact there's
no reason why it shouldn't work equally well with some of the tender, early summer
vegetables, such as young carrots, courgettes (zucchini) and French (fine green) beans.

serves 4

Soak, rinse and cook the beans as usual, then drain them,
reserving the cooking liquid. Make the liquid up to
400ml/14fl oz/1¾ cups with the milk.

    Peel and dice the carrots and swede (rutabaga). Clean
and slice the leeks and celery. Peel and slice the onions.
Cook all the vegetables together in boiling salted water
until they're just tender, then drain them.

    Melt the butter in a good-sized saucepan and stir in
the flour. When it 'froths', draw the saucepan off the heat
and stir in the cooking liquid and milk, then return the
saucepan to the heat and stir until the sauce thickens. Let
the sauce simmer gently for about 10 minutes, to cook
the flour, then stir in half the cheese, the beans and the
cooked vegetables. Season with sea salt and freshly
ground black pepper. Turn the mixture into a shallow
casserole, sprinkle with the crumbs and remaining cheese,
and make hot and brown under the grill (broiler).

175g/6oz/scant 1 cup
butter or lima beans
150–300ml/5–10fl oz/
⅔–1¼ cups milk
225g/8oz carrots
225g/8oz swede (rutabaga)
225g/8oz leeks
4 celery stalks
4 onions
sea salt
40g/1½oz/3tbsp butter
40g/1½oz/4½tbsp flour
125g/4oz/1 cup grated
cheese
freshly ground black pepper
wholewheat breadcrumbs

chick peas with garlic

This is my version of a Lebanese chick pea (garbanzo bean) dish. It's cheap and simple, but very good.

serves 4

350g/12oz/1¾ cups chick peas (garbanzo beans)
3 large cloves garlic, crushed
sea salt
freshly ground black pepper
olive oil
4 slices of stale bread

To serve
wedges of lemon
paprika

Soak the chick peas (garbanzo beans), then drain and rinse them and cook in fresh water as usual. Drain them, reserving their cooking water. Mash the chick peas (garbanzo beans), or pass them through a food mill. Alternatively, whizz them in the food processor or blender, adding some of their cooking water if necessary, to make a smooth, fairly thick purée. Flavour this purée with the garlic and add some sea salt, freshly ground black pepper and a couple of tablespoonfuls of olive oil to taste. Reheat the mixture and keep it warm.

Cut the stale bread into small dice and fry them in a little olive oil – or, if you want to economize, vegetable oil – until they're crisp.

Serve the purée topped with a little more olive oil and scatter the fried bread pieces on top. Garnish with wedges of lemon and some paprika.

cocido

There are many versions of this Spanish dish, containing varying quantities of meat. As a vegetarian, I prefer to make this more modest version, without meat, although strictly speaking a piece of salt pork or bacon, weighing 125–175g/4–6oz, should be included. Some of the more complicated cocidos are served as three courses: first the liquid is strained off, mixed with vermicelli and served as soup; then the chick peas (garbanzo beans) and vegetables are removed from the saucepan for the next course; finally, the meat is served. This simple cocido is best served in one bowl as a stew, with some bread or croûtons.

serves 4

Soak, drain and rinse the chick peas (garbanzo beans) as usual. Put them into a large saucepan, cover them generously with vegetable stock and simmer them for about 1 hour, until they're almost tender. Meanwhile, peel the potatoes and cut them into even-sized chunks. Peel and slice the onions, carrots and turnip. Wash the leeks thoroughly and cut into slices. Wash and quarter the cabbage and crush the garlic. Add the vegetables to the chick peas (garbanzo beans) in the saucepan, together with the paprika, bouquet garni, oil and a little more stock if you think it necessary. Simmer gently for a further 30 minutes or so until everything is done. Remove the bouquet garni; season the mixture with sea salt and freshly ground black pepper.

350g/12oz/1¾ cups chick peas (garbanzo beans)
vegetable stock
3 potatoes
2 onions
2 carrots
1 turnip
2 leeks
1 small cabbage
2 cloves garlic
1tbsp paprika
bouquet garni – a couple of sprigs of parsley, a sprig of thyme and a bayleaf, tied together
2tbsp oil
sea salt
freshly ground black pepper

lentils and spinach

You might think this is a most unpromising combination, but it works well, and is so soothing to eat I don't wonder it was served to the Persian sick in the Middle Ages.

serves 4

450g/1lb spinach
225g/8oz/heaping 1 cup green lentils, soaked and cooked until tender, then drained
1 onion, peeled and chopped
2 cloves garlic, crushed
25g/1oz/2tbsp butter
good pinch each of ground cumin and ground coriander
sea salt
freshly ground black pepper
juice of ½ lemon

Wash the spinach carefully by putting it into a big bowl of cold water and swishing it round, then draining it and repeating twice more. Shred it roughly, then put it into a dry saucepan. Cook over a moderate heat, with a lid on the saucepan, until it's tender – about 10 minutes. Drain off the liquid which will have accumulated. Add the cooked drained lentils to the spinach and have the saucepan over a gentle heat to keep the spinach hot and heat the lentils through.

Fry the onion and garlic in the butter for 10 minutes, until tender, then stir in the spices and cook for a minute or two longer. Add this mixture to the spinach and lentils, together with sea salt and freshly ground black pepper to taste, and the lemon juice. Serve at once.

This dish looks attractive garnished with some wedges of hardboiled egg, yellow and white against bright green, but it's also very good served just as it is, perhaps with some slices of brown bread and butter.

lentil and split pea casserole

serves 4

Wash the lentils and split peas and put them into a saucepan with 900ml/1½ pints/3¾ cups of the stock. Bring them to the boil, then turn the heat down and leave them to simmer gently until tender, about 30 minutes.

Meanwhile, prepare the vegetables. Wash the leeks thoroughly and cut them into 2.5 cm/1 inch slices. Peel and chop the onions. Peel the parsnips and carrots and cut them into chunky dice. Melt the butter in a large flameproof casserole or saucepan and add all the vegetables. Fry them for 5 minutes, stirring them often so that they all get well coated with the fat, but don't let them brown. Add the flour and mix well, then pour in the rest of the stock and the cooked lentils and peas, together with any of their liquid. Season well with sea salt and freshly ground black pepper. Cover the saucepan and cook gently for about 30 minutes, until all the vegetables are tender. Sprinkle with the grated cheese before serving.

75g/3oz/scant ½ cup split red lentils

75g/3oz/heaping ⅓ cup split peas

1.5 litres/2⅓ pints/1½ quarts well-flavoured vegetable stock

450g/1lb leeks

2 large onions

225g/8oz parsnips

225g/8oz carrots

50g/2oz/¼ cup butter

1 tbsp flour

sea salt

freshly ground black pepper

125g/4oz/1 cup grated cheese

frijoles refritos

Though popularly known as re-fried beans, they are in fact twice-cooked – first in water, then in the frying pan.

serves 4

350g/12oz/2 cups red kidney beans
1.2 litres/2 pints/1¼ quarts water
3 large onions, peeled and chopped
3 cloves garlic, crushed
75g/3oz/6tbsp butter
¼–½tsp chilli powder
400g/14oz can tomatoes
sea salt
chopped fresh coriander (cilantro)

To serve
tortillas or crusty garlic bread

Soak, drain and rinse the beans as usual. Put the beans into a saucepan with the cold water, one of the chopped onions, one of the crushed cloves of garlic, a quarter of the butter and the chilli powder. Bring them up to the boil and boil vigorously for 10 minutes, then simmer them gently for about 1 hour, with a lid on the saucepan, until the beans are tender and the liquid absorbed.

Now for the frying part. Melt the remaining butter in another large saucepan and fry the rest of the onion and garlic for about 10 minutes, until the onion is soft, then add the tomatoes and simmer for 2–3 minutes. Mix the beans into the onion and tomatoes a couple of spoonfuls at a time, mashing them roughly as you do so. When all the beans have been added, cook the mixture gently for about 10 minutes to heat everything through. Taste for seasoning, sprinkle with coriander (cilantro) and serve with tortillas or crusty garlic bread.

root vegetable and lentil stew

Real warming winter food, this: root vegetables with pulses (legumes), and very filling and satisfying too. You can add whatever herbs and spices you fancy; my suggestion of ground coriander and cumin makes it spicy without being hot.

serves 3–4

Heat 2tbsp of the oil in a large saucepan and put in the root vegetables, onion and celery. Fry the vegetables in the oil, without browning them, for about 5 minutes, then add the lentils and garlic and cook them all gently for a further 4–5 minutes, stirring often. Mix in the tomatoes and stock, put a lid on the saucepan and leave it to simmer away gently for about 30 minutes, until all the vegetables are tender and the lentils pale golden and soft. Meanwhile, fry the extra onion in the remaining oil for 10 minutes, then add the ground coriander and cumin and fry for a further minute or two to draw out the flavour of the spices. Stir this mixture into the cooked lentils, then add sea salt and freshly ground black pepper to taste and the lemon juice. Scatter with a little chopped parsley before serving. If you prefer to cook this in the oven, it takes about an hour towards the bottom at 200°C/ 400°F/Gas 6.

3tbsp oil
750g/1½lb mixed root vegetables, peeled and diced
1 large onion, peeled and chopped
2 celery stalks, sliced
175g/6oz/scant 1 cup split red lentils
2 cloves garlic, crushed
225g/8oz/1 cup canned tomatoes
750ml/1¼ pints/3 cups vegetable stock

To finish
1 onion, peeled and chopped
1–2tsp ground coriander
1–2tsp ground cumin
sea salt
freshly ground black pepper
juice of ½ lemon
a little chopped fresh parsley

vegetable dishes

As you may have gathered, pulses (legumes) can stand on their own, happily playing the leading role in the meal and supplying necessary nutrients. However, they're also useful for 'stretching' other more expensive proteins, which can then be served in much smaller quantities. Pease pudding, used by generations of thrifty housewives in the north of England to help eke out the precious Sunday roast, is an example of this, although I must admit that as a vegetarian I like to serve pease pudding with a good gravy, golden roast potatoes, mint sauce and green vegetables.

Don't be put off serving pulses (legumes) as a vegetable by memories of school dinner butter beans, all dreary beige dullness. It's surprising what a little tender loving care, plus some garlic, butter, cream and herbs, can do to transform them into something far from dull.

beans in leek sauce

The mixture of leeks and beans is a good one and in this recipe they combine to make a creamy, protein-rich supper dish. I think this needs something crisp to go with it – fried bread, or crunchy fried potatoes.

serves 3–4

Soak, cook and drain the beans as usual, reserving 300ml/10fl oz/1¼ cups of the cooking water for the sauce. Wash the leeks thoroughly, and cut them into thin slices. Melt the butter and fry the leeks in it until they're soft and lightly browned, then stir in the flour and cook together for 1–2 minutes. Mix in the bean liquid and milk and cook until boiling, stirring constantly until the mixture is smooth and thick. Simmer very gently for 10 minutes. Add the grated cheese and beans and season to taste. Reheat the beans before serving.

225g/8oz/heaping 1 cup haricot (navy) beans
2 leeks
50g/2oz/¼ cup butter
50g/2oz/6tbsp plain (all-purpose) flour
300ml/10fl oz/1¼ cups milk
125g/4oz/1 cup grated cheese
sea salt
freshly ground black pepper

beans and mushrooms

If you feel this dish is rather on the rich side, you could omit the cream.

serves 4

175g/6oz/scant 1 cup butter or lima beans
225g/8oz/3 cups young white button mushrooms
25g/1oz/2tbsp butter
1tbsp lemon juice
150ml/5fl oz/⅔ cup double (heavy) cream
sea salt
freshly ground black pepper
grated nutmeg
1tbsp chopped fresh parsley

Soak, drain and rinse the beans as usual. Put them into a saucepan, cover with water and cook until tender. Drain and keep them warm.

Wash the mushrooms and halve or quarter them if necessary. Fry them gently in the butter in a medium-sized saucepan for 2–3 minutes until they're just tender, then stir in the beans, lemon juice and cream. Season to taste with sea salt, freshly ground black pepper and grated nutmeg. Serve sprinkled with chopped parsley.

butter beans with tomatoes, mint and olive oil

This is a Greek recipe, and the result is moist, rich and flavoursome. The beans can be served as a vegetable, or with rice. I think they make a lovely supper dish with home-made wholewheat rolls and a green salad. They're also very good cold, especially if you throw in a few black olives too. Lima beans can be used instead of the butter beans if you prefer.

serves 4 as a main protein dish, 8 as a vegetable

Soak, drain and rinse the beans as usual. Put them into a saucepan with fresh cold water, bring them up to the boil and simmer until tender.

While all this is happening, peel the onions and chop them finely; crush the garlic. Fry the onions in the olive oil in a good-sized saucepan for 10 minutes, allowing them to brown lightly, then stir in the garlic. Chop the tomatoes and add these to the saucepan, together with the cooked and drained beans, the mint and some sea salt and freshly ground black pepper. Let the mixture simmer gently, covered, for about 20 minutes, to allow all the flavours to blend. Taste and add more sea salt and freshly ground black pepper, and a little sugar if you think it's necessary.

450g/1lb/2¼ cups butter beans
3 large onions
2 cloves garlic
150ml/5fl oz/⅔ cup olive oil
400g/14oz can tomatoes
2tbsp chopped fresh mint
sea salt
freshly ground black pepper
a little sugar

revithia yahni

This simple chick pea (garbanzo bean) purée from Greece can be flavoured with as much parsley and mint as you like: it can take plenty. It's also good cold.

serves 4–6

450g/1lb/scant 2¼ cups chick peas (garbanzo beans)
4 large onions, peeled and chopped
3 cloves garlic, crushed
4tbsp olive oil
400g/14oz can tomatoes
2–4tbsp chopped fresh parsley
2–4tbsp chopped fresh mint
lemon juice
sea salt
freshly ground black pepper

To serve
crusty bread
olive oil

Soak, drain and rinse the chick peas (garbanzo beans) as usual. Put them into a saucepan with a good covering of cold water and cook them gently until they're very tender. Drain and purée the chick peas (garbanzo beans) by whizzing them in the food processor or blender with some of their cooking liquor – but don't make them too sloppy. Alternatively, they can be passed through a food mill.

Fry the onions and garlic in the oil for 10 minutes, then add the tomatoes and cook for a further 5 minutes. Stir in the puréed chick peas (garbanzo beans), parsley and mint, and flavour with lemon juice, sea salt and freshly ground black pepper. Put over a gentle heat until everything is nice and hot, then serve with crusty bread and hand round olive oil.

chick peas with sweet peppers and tomatoes

This is a simple dish which is good served as a vegetable, or with just a tossed green salad and some warm rolls and butter for a simple meal, with fruit and yogurt to follow. It's also delicious cold, particularly if you can stir in a few black olives and some extra olive oil.

serves 4

Soak, rinse and cook the chick peas (garbanzo beans) as usual. Meanwhile, peel and slice the onions and crush the garlic, then fry them gently in the olive oil until they're tender, about 10 minutes. Halve the red peppers and remove the seeds, then slice the peppers thinly and add them to the onions and garlic. Cook for 5 minutes, then stir in the canned tomatoes, tomato paste and chilli powder and cook gently for 10 minutes.

Drain the chick peas (garbanzo beans), add them to the vegetables and heat through gently. Season with sea salt and freshly ground black pepper, and add a little sugar if you think the mixture needs it. Serve garnished with the chopped parsley.

225g/8oz/heaping 1 cup chick peas (garbanzo beans)
2 large onions
2 large cloves garlic
4tbsp olive oil
2 sweet red peppers
225g/8oz/1 cup canned tomatoes
1tbsp tomato paste
½tsp chilli powder
sea salt
freshly ground black pepper
a little sugar to taste

To serve
2tbsp chopped fresh parsley

chick peas in tomato sauce

This nice, spicy mixture is also good served with buttered pasta.

serves 4

225g/8oz/heaping 1 cup chick peas (garbanzo beans)
1 small onion
25g/1oz/2tbsp butter
1 clove garlic, crushed
125g/4oz/1½ cups button mushrooms, wiped and sliced
400g/14oz can tomatoes
1 bayleaf
sea salt
freshly ground black pepper
¼–½tsp chilli powder
a little sugar

Soak, drain, rinse and cook the chick peas (garbanzo beans) as usual. When they're soft, drain them and set them aside while you make the sauce.

Peel and chop the onion and fry it gently in the butter in a medium-sized saucepan for 5 minutes; don't let it brown. Then stir in the garlic and mushrooms and fry for a further 5 minutes. Add the tomatoes and bayleaf and cook over a moderate heat for 10–15 minutes, until most of the liquid has boiled away, leaving a nice thick sauce. Season with sea salt, freshly ground black pepper and chilli powder, also a little sugar if you think it needs it. Then mix in the chick peas (garbanzo beans) and cook for a further few minutes to heat them through. Check seasoning before serving.

chilli red beans

Red beans cooked with onion, garlic, tomatoes and chilli make a spicy and unusual vegetable dish, and add protein as well as colour to a meal.

serves 4

Soak, drain, rinse and cook the beans as usual, boiling them vigorously for the first 10 minutes.

Fry the onion and garlic in the oil in a large saucepan for 10 minutes, then add the tomatoes, chilli powder and the cooked and drained beans. Simmer gently for 10 minutes, to heat through and let the flavours blend. Season with salt and freshly ground black pepper.

225g/8oz/1⅓ cups red kidney beans
1 large onion, peeled and chopped
1 large clove garlic, crushed
2tbsp oil
400g/14oz can tomatoes
½–1tsp chilli powder
sea salt
freshly ground black pepper

dried peas with mint and cream

If you want a smoother finish to this dish, the peas can be passed through a food mill before any of the other ingredients are added. I think this improves them.

serves 4

225g/8oz/ heaping 1 cup whole dried peas
25g/1oz/2tbsp butter
1 small onion, peeled and chopped
2tbsp chopped fresh mint
2–3tbsp cream
sea salt
freshly ground black pepper
sugar

Soak, rinse and drain the peas as usual, then cover them with water and simmer them until they're very tender. Drain the peas; keep them warm.

Melt the butter and fry the onion lightly until it's soft but not browned. Add the onion and butter to the peas, also the mint, cream and seasoning, including a little sugar if you think the mixture needs it.

white beans with celery

The flavours of haricot (navy) beans and celery go well together, but as they're very much the same colour, you do need the parsley to give colour to the dish.

serves 4

Cover the beans with water and cook them gently until they're soft. While this is happening, wash the celery thoroughly, discarding tough outer stalks. Cut the rest into even-sized pieces and cook in boiling salted water until they're tender. Drain the celery and the beans and mix them together; add the butter and sea salt and freshly ground black pepper. Sprinkle with chopped parsley and serve at once.

175g/6oz/scant 1 cup
haricot (navy) beans,
soaked, drained and rinsed
2 small bunches of celery
sea salt
25g/1oz/2tbsp butter
freshly ground black pepper

To serve
2 good tbsp chopped fresh
parsley

white beans with cream and herbs

This recipe shows how simple it is to transform plain beans into something special.

serves 4–6

225g/8oz/heaping 1 cup
haricot (navy) or butter
beans
25g/1oz/2tbsp butter
150ml/5fl oz/⅔ cup cream
2–3tsp lemon juice
2tbsp chopped fresh green
herbs – parsley, chives,
tarragon – as available
sea salt
freshly ground black pepper
grated nutmeg

Soak, drain, rinse and cook the beans as usual, then drain them. While they're still hot, add the butter, cream, a little lemon juice to taste, and the green herbs. Season carefully with sea salt, freshly ground black pepper and nutmeg. Reheat gently, just enough to make everything nice and hot – don't let it boil. Serve immediately.

white beans in tomato sauce

This dish comes from Provence, where it is often served with lamb.

Peel and finely chop the onion; crush the garlic. Heat the oil in a medium-sized saucepan over a moderate heat, add the onion and garlic and cook them gently until the onion has softened but not browned. Stir in the cooked beans and tomatoes. Bring the mixture to the boil, stirring continuously and breaking up the tomatoes as you do so. Stir in the oregano. Let the mixture simmer for about 15 minutes, without a lid on the saucepan, to reduce the liquid a bit. Season with sea salt and freshly ground black pepper, and serve sprinkled with chopped parsley.

serves 4–6

1 large onion
1–2 cloves garlic
2tbsp oil
400g/14oz can tomatoes
225g/8oz/heaping 1 cup
haricot (navy) beans,
soaked, cooked and drained
1tsp dried oregano
sea salt
freshly ground black pepper

To serve
1tbsp chopped fresh parsley

pease pudding

serves 4

225g/8oz/1 cup yellow split peas

1 large onion, peeled and chopped

50g/2oz/¼ cup butter

1 egg

sea salt

freshly ground black pepper

Soak, drain and rinse the split peas as usual. Put them into a saucepan with cold water just to cover. Simmer the split peas gently until they're tender, then drain off any excess water.

Fry the onion in the butter for about 10 minutes, until it's soft, then add it to the cooked split peas, together with the egg, and sea salt and freshly ground black pepper to taste. Put the mixture into a greased bowl with a covering of foil and steam it for 1 hour.

Alternatively, spoon it into a greased casserole dish and bake it in a moderate oven, 180°C/350°F/Gas 4, for about 30 minutes.

purée of flageolets

A delicate pale green purée of flageolets is very useful when you want to add extra protein to the meal.

serves 4

Soak, drain and rinse the beans as usual, then cover them with fresh cold water and simmer them gently until tender. Drain, reserving the cooking liquid.

While the beans are cooking, fry the onion gently in the butter until it is soft but not browned – about 10 minutes.

Whizz the beans in the food processor or blender with the cream and onion mixture, and enough of the reserved cooking liquor if necessary to make a smooth purée. Alternatively, pass the beans through a food mill, then mix with the cream, onion mixture and a little cooking liquor. Season with sea salt, freshly ground black pepper and grated nutmeg. Reheat gently, but don't let the mixture boil, and serve garnished with chopped parsley.

225g/8oz/heaping 1 cup flageolet beans
1 small onion, peeled and chopped
25g/1oz/2tbsp butter
4–6tbsp single (light) cream
sea salt
freshly ground black pepper
grated nutmeg

To serve
1tbsp finely chopped fresh parsley

two bean vegetable dish

I like the way the French serve dried beans with fresh green beans in such dishes as pistou and aïgroissade. It's an idea that works well in a simple vegetable dish too, and the contrasting shades of green make this mixture attractive to the eye as well.

serves 4

175g/6oz/scant 1 cup flageolet beans
450g/1lb French (fine green) beans
sea salt
25g/1oz/2tbsp butter
freshly ground black pepper
1tbsp chopped fresh parsley
1tbsp chopped fresh summer savory – if available, otherwise use other green herbs such as chives, tarragon or extra parsley

Soak, drain and rinse the flageolets as usual, then cook them in fresh cold water until they're soft. Drain and keep them warm. Top and tail the French (fine green) beans and cut them into short lengths. Cook them in a little boiling salted water until they're tender, then drain them and add them to the cooked flageolets, together with the butter. Check the seasoning, then add the fresh herbs just before serving.

yellow split pea purée with vegetables

This recipe is from Germany, and is not unlike our pease pudding. I think some triangles of crisp fried bread go well with it, or crunchy fried potatoes.

serves 4

Soak the split peas in water for an hour or two, then drain and rinse them and put them into a saucepan with the water, half the sliced onions and all the other vegetables and herbs. Let them simmer gently until the split peas are soft and the vegetables tender – about 30 minutes. Sieve the mixture or whizz it in the food processor or blender, then season it with lemon juice, sea salt and freshly ground black pepper. Spoon the mixture into a shallow flameproof dish. Fry the remaining onion in the butter until it's beginning to soften, then pour the onion and the butter over the top of the purée. Put the purée under a fairly hot grill (broiler) until the top is slightly crusted looking and the onion very crisp and brown.

225g/8oz/1 cup yellow split peas
600ml/1 pint/2½ cups water
2 medium onions, peeled and sliced
1 medium carrot, scraped and sliced
1 small leek, cleaned and sliced
1 celery stalk, sliced
good pinch of dried mint or marjoram
1tbsp lemon juice
sea salt
freshly ground black pepper
40g/1½oz/3tbsp butter

basic recipes

white sauce

If you like, you can give this basic white sauce extra flavour by adding a bayleaf or a bouquet garni. Simmer these in the milk for a minute or two, then leave them in the hot milk for 15 minutes, taking them out before using the milk to make the sauce.

Melt the butter in a medium-sized saucepan, stir in the flour and let it cook for a minute or two, but don't let it brown. Remove the pan from the heat and add the milk. I use a small balloon whisk for this and if you also heat the milk, you'll always have a nice smooth sauce. When you've added the milk, put the saucepan back over the heat and go on whisking as the sauce thickens, then turn the heat down and let the sauce simmer very gently for 15 minutes to cook the flour and reduce the sauce to the right consistency. Season with sea salt, freshly ground black pepper and nutmeg to taste.

25g/1oz/2tbsp butter
25g/1oz/3tbsp plain (all-purpose) flour
400ml/14fl oz/1¾ cups milk, preferably hot
sea salt
freshly ground black pepper
grated nutmeg

cheese sauce

Add 125g/4oz/1 cup grated Cheddar cheese after removing the sauce from the heat when it has thickened and cooked. Use less salt, because of the cheese.

quick blender method

Simply blend the butter, flour, milk, about ½tsp sea salt and a good grinding of black pepper at high speed for a few seconds. There will be some lumpy bits of butter, but that doesn't matter. Stir over a moderate heat until the sauce has thickened, then simmer gently for 15 minutes.

quick blender parsley sauce

Put some sprigs of parsley into the blender with the other ingredients at the beginning of the process.

tomato sauce

This is a very useful basic sauce which can be varied with different flavourings.

1tbsp oil
1 onion, peeled and chopped
2 cloves garlic, crushed
400g/14oz can tomatoes
in juice, chopped
sea salt
freshly ground black pepper

Heat the oil in a medium-sized saucepan, add the onion, stir, then cover the pan and let the onion cook gently for about 7 minutes. Stir in the garlic and cook for a minute or two, then put in the tomatoes. Leave to boil gently for 10–15 minutes, until the mixture is thick and purée-like. Season with salt and freshly ground black pepper.

This basic tomato sauce can be made hotter by the addition of a little chilli powder or cayenne pepper; or try it with a teaspoonful of grated fresh ginger added with the garlic, some crushed coriander seeds, grated lemon rind, or a glass of red wine added with the tomatoes.

crêpes

I usually make this batter in the food processor or blender, but you can equally well use the traditional method. Both methods are given here. For best results with either method, I use a half-and-half mix of wholewheat and white flours.

makes 10–12 crêpes

For the food processor or blender method, put all the ingredients in and whizz at medium speed for 1–2 minutes to make a smooth, creamy batter. For the traditional method, sift the flour and salt into a bowl, make a well in the centre and add the eggs, the oil and about a third of the milk. Mix to a smooth consistency, gradually adding the remaining milk, then beat well for 1–2 minutes.

Whichever method you use, leave the batter to stand for 30 minutes before using it, then beat it again lightly.

To fry the crêpes, set a small frying pan over a low heat and coat the inside with oil using kitchen paper. When the pan is hot, pour in about 2 tbsp batter – enough to coat the base of the pan thinly – and swirl it round so that the base of the pan is covered. Fry for a minute or two, until the base of the crêpe is cooked, then flip the crêpe over to cook the other side. When that's done, lift out the crêpe and put it on a plate while you make the rest. Brush the pan with oil before making each crêpe, and pile them on top of each other on the plate as they're done.

Crêpes freeze very well: wrap the pile of cooled crêpes in foil and put them in the freezer. When you want to use them, loosen the foil and thaw them out naturally, or put the foil parcel in a low oven. They will also keep for several days in the fridge.

125g/4oz/¾ cup + 2tbsp plain (all-purpose) flour
¼tsp sea salt
2 medium eggs
2tbsp vegetable oil
200ml/7fl oz/ scant 1 cup milk

For frying
oil

pastry

This is my favourite recipe for shortcrust (pie) pastry. In traditional recipes, the quantity of pastry is conventionally given by the weight of the flour: pastry made from 200g/7oz flour would be described as 200g/7oz pastry. However, now that ready made pastry is often substituted, I think it is clearer to give the actual weight of the finished pastry, as I have done here. I like to make this pastry from a half-and-half mix of wholewheat and white flour, which gives a lovely nutty flavour, appetizing light brown colour and the health benefits of wholewheat flour – at the same time as keeping the pastry light in texture.

makes about
320g/11oz

200g/7oz/1¼ cups plain wholewheat flour or a half-and-half mix of plain white (all-purpose) flour and wholewheat flour

½tsp salt

100g/3½oz/scant ½ cup butter, roughly chopped

about 2½tbsp cold water

Put the flour, salt, butter and water into a food processor and whizz just until a dough forms – don't overblend. Alternatively, put the dry ingredients in a bowl, rub in the butter with your fingertips until the mixture resembles breadcrumbs, then mix in just enough water to make a dough. Knead the dough very lightly on a lightly floured board and roll out as required.

index

adzuki beans xiii, xxv
   Japanese red-cooked rice 110
aïgroissade 21
aubergines (eggplant):
   musakka'a 60
   stuffed with chick peas 120
   stuffed with lentils and mushrooms 121

bean:
   apple and beetroot salad 23
   and carrot soup 2
   and fresh herb spread 40
   and garlic spread 40
   and herb salad 41
   and leek pie 92
   and olive spread 40
   and onion quiche 95
   paella 102
   and parsley spread 40
   pepper and tomato quiche 97
   tomato and onion salad 25
   and tomato pie 93
   and vegetable curry 104
   and vegetable gratin 135
   and vegetable pie 56
   and watercress soup 12
   and wheat casserole 103
bean sprouts xvi
beans:
   in leek sauce 143
   with marrow and corn 131
   and mushrooms 144
   and mushrooms with coriander (salad) 24
beany:
   goulash 132
   salad bowl 22
   Scotch eggs 65
beorijch 133
black beans xiii, xxv
black eyed beans xiii, xxv
   bake 52
   beorijch 133
   with marrow and corn 131
   shepherds' beany pie 62
   and vegetable stew 134
borlotti beans xiii–xiv, xxv

Boston baked beans 53
British field beans xxv
broad beans xiv, xxv
   aïgroissade 21
bulgur wheat, and bean casserole 103
burgers:
   lentil and egg 70
   spicy lentil 73
butter beans xiv, xxv
   baked, and cheese 51
   bean, apple and beetroot salad 23
   bean and leek pie 92
   bean and onion quiche 95
   bean, tomato and onion salad 25
   bean and tomato pie 93
   beans and mushrooms 144
   beans and mushrooms with coriander 24
   beany salad bowl 22
   creamy bean dip 34
   soup, cream of 7
   spaghetti and bean bake 90
   and tomato soup 3
   with tomatoes, mint and olive oil 145
   and vegetable curry 104
   and vegetable gratin 135
   white beans with cream and herbs 152

cabbage and bean salad 26
canned beans, quantity vi
cannellini beans xiv, xxv
   apple and celery salad 27
   beany goulash 132
cheese sauce 159
chick peas (garbanzo beans) xiv, xxv
   aïgroissade 21
   apple and leek salad 28
   aubergines stuffed with 120
   beany salad bowl 22
   cocido 137
   courgettes with chick pea and mushroom stuffing 122
   curried 105
   felafel 67
   with garlic 136
   hot stuffed tomatoes 127
   hummus 43

musakka'a 60
and mushroom quiche 96
nibbles 29
and potato croquettes 66
revithia yahni 146
with rice and tomatoes 113
salad 30
and salad with yogurt 31
sopa de panela 18
with sweet peppers and tomatoes 147
three bean salad 49
in tomato sauce 148
tuoni e lampo 85
chilled split pea soup with mint 4
chilli:
red bean crêpes 79
red beans 149
cocido 137
courgettes with chick pea and mushroom stuffing 122
creamy bean dip 34
crêpes 78–84
batter & preparation 161
croquettes:
chick pea and potato 66
lentil and cheese, with tomato sauce 69
soya bean and egg 74
curried lentil and pineapple salad 35
curried lentil spread 36
curries:
bean and vegetable 104
chick pea 105
lentil:
and pineapple 106
quick 112
simple 115
mung dal 107
red kidney bean 108
soya bean 116

dal 109
soup 9
split pea, with hardboiled eggs 117
dried beans, quantity vi
dried peas:
green pea fritters 68
with mint and cream 150

equipment xix–xx

fasolada 10

fava beans see broad beans
fazolia beans see cannellini beans
felafel 67
fennel and lentil au gratin 55
flageolet beans xv, xxv
and avocado salad 37
and button mushroom salad 38
cold stuffed tomatoes 128
crêpes with flageolet, mushroom and
artichoke heart filling 80
and onion salad 39
purée 155
soup 11
two bean vegetable dish 156
freezing xxiv, 161
French (fine green) beans:
aïgroissade 21
two bean vegetable dish 156
frijoles refritos 140
fritters, split pea, with apple rings 75
ful medames beans xv, xxv

garbanzo beans see chick peas
goulash, beany 132
Greek bean salad 42
green beans see French beans
green pea fritters 68

haricot (navy) beans xv, xxv
bean and carrot soup 2
beans in leek sauce 143
beany goulash 132
Boston baked beans 53
cream of white bean soup 8
fasolada 10
and garlic spread 40
Greek bean salad 42
and herb salad 41
pepper and tomato quiche 97
pistou 16
ratatouille 130
spaghetti and bean bake 90
three bean salad 49
vegetable pie 56
and watercress soup 12
and wheat casserole 103
white beans with celery 151
white beans with cream and herbs 152
white beans in tomato sauce 153
hummus 43

Indian rice crêpes with split pea filling 82–3

Japanese red-cooked rice 110

khitchari 111
kidney beans see red kidney beans

lasagne, lentil 89
lentils:
    brown xvi, xxv
    green xvi, xxv
        aubergines stuffed with lentils and
            mushrooms 121
        bean and wheat casserole 103
        beany Scotch eggs 65
        crêpes with spinach and lentil filling 84
        curried, simple 115
        and egg bake 57
        and egg burgers 70
        lasagne 89
        and mushroom pâté 32
        and mushroom soup 5
        salad, Mediterranean 33
        sauce, for spaghetti 86
        shepherds' lentil pie 63
        spicy burgers 73
        and spinach 138
        and spinach soup 19
        stuffed mushroom caps 123
        stuffed onions 124
        sweet peppers with lentil and tomato
            stuffing 126
        toad-in-the-hole 54
        and vegetable soup 6
        and walnut loaf 76
    Puy xvi, xxv
    split red xvi, xxv, 64
        bean and wheat casserole 103
        and cheese croquettes 69
        and chive spread 44
        crêpes with lentil and mushroom
            filling 81
        curried:
            and pineapple 106
            and pineapple salad 35
            spread 36
        curry, quick 112
        dal 109
        dal soup 9
        fennel and lentil au gratin 55

    and green pepper quiche 98
    and mushroom slice 58
    and onion rissoles with mint sauce 71
    pastichio 88
    rissoles with yogurt sauce 72
    and root vegetable stew 141
    shurit ads 14
    soup 17
        with curried croûtons 13
    and spinach casserole 59
    and split pea casserole 139
    tomato and mushroom quiche 99
    and tomato pie 94
    and tomato sauce, for spaghetti 87
    and tomato soup 15
    and tomato spread 44
lima beans xvi, xxv
    bean, apple and beetroot salad 23
    bean and leek pie 92
    bean and onion quiche 95
    bean, tomato and onion salad 25
    bean and tomato pie 93
    beans and mushrooms 144
    beans and mushrooms with coriander 24
    beany salad bowl 22
    creamy bean dip 34
    spaghetti and bean bake 90
    and vegetable gratin 135

masur dal xvi
Mediterranean lentil salad 33
mung beans xvi, xxv
    curried mung dal 107
    khitchari 111
musakka'a 60

navy beans see haricot beans

paella 102
pasta 85–90
pastichio 88
pastry 162
peas xvii, xxv
    see also dried peas; split peas
pease pudding 154
pinto beans xvii, xxv
pistou 16
pressure cooking xix, xxiii
protein xi–xii
Puy lentils xvi, xxv

quiches:
    bean, pepper and tomato 97
    bean and onion 95
    chick pea and mushroom 96
    lentil and green pepper 98
    lentil, tomato and mushroom 99
    red bean and tomato 100
quick blender parsley sauce 159
quick blender white sauce 159
quick lentil curry 112

ratatouille 130
re-fried beans 140
red kidney beans xvii
    preparation xxiii–xxiv
    chilli red bean crêpes 79
    chilli red beans 149
    curried 108
    frijoles refritos 140
    red bean moussaka 61
    red bean and orange salad 45
    red bean salad 46
    red bean and tomato quiche 100
    rice and bean salad 47
    rice and peas 114
    Russian red beans with damson sauce 48
    stuffed sweet peppers 125
    three bean salad 49
    West Indian red beans 118
revithia yahni 146
rice:
    bean paella 102
    and bean salad 47
    with chick peas and tomatoes 113
    Indian rice crêpes with split pea filling
      83–4
    Japanese red-cooked 110
    khitchari 111
    and peas 114
rissoles 64
    lentil, with yogurt sauce 72
    lentil and onion, with mint sauce 71
root vegetable and lentil stew 141
Russian red beans with damson sauce 48

sauces 159
Scotch eggs, beany 65
shepherds' beany pie 62
shepherds' lentil pie 63
shortcrust pastry 162

shurit ads 14
slow cooking pots xix, xxiii
soaking, method xxii
sopa de panela 18
soups 1–19
soya beans xvii, xxv
    curry 116
    and egg croquettes 74
    loaf 77
soybeans see soya beans
spaghetti:
    and bean bake 90
    with green lentil sauce 86
    with lentil and tomato sauce 87
spicy lentil burgers 73
spinach and lentil soup 19
split peas xviii, xxv, 64
    dal, with hardboiled eggs 117
    dal soup 9
    fritters, with apple rings 75
    Indian rice crêpes with split pea filling 82–3
    and lentil casserole 139
    pease pudding 154
    soup, chilled, with mint 4
    yellow split pea purée with vegetables 157
storage xix, xxiv
stuffed mushroom caps 123
stuffed onions 124
stuffed sweet peppers 125, 126
stuffed tomatoes:
    cold 128
    hot 127
sweet peppers with lentil and tomato stuffing 126

three bean salad 49
toad-in-the-hole, lentil 54
tomato sauce 160
tuoni e lampo 85
two bean vegetable dish 156

washing, method xxi–xxii
West Indian red beans 118
white beans:
    with celery 151
    with cream and herbs 152
    soup, cream of 8
    in tomato sauce 153
white sauce 159

yellow split pea purée with vegetables 157